ENDORSEMENTS

Excellent blend of testimony, truth, and hope for change through intimate communion with Jesus and His body. Williams makes a smart
and compassionate case for laying aside LGBTQ+ identification for
the feast of knowing Jesus and one's true self. His life and his book
fuse hope with the hardships implicit in forging Christian maturity,
which Williams himself exemplifies.

Andrew Comiskey
Executive Director, Desert Stream Ministries
Author of *Pursuing Sexual Wholeness*

If homosexuality has felt like an intimidating topic, as it has for many
believers, here is the book we have been waiting for. In *The Journey OUT*,
Ken Williams discusses same-sex attraction with wisdom, compassion,
and—most importantly—God's loving truth. He shares his own journey
of sexual healing alongside testimonies of God's total transformation
in the lives of many others. This book is not only for people who want
freedom from same-sex attraction; it will empower every reader with
a greater understanding and an unshakeable hope of God's goodness
and His plan for redemption in one of the greatest cultural issues of
our day. *The Journey OUT* could not have come at a better time.

Bill Johnson
Senior Leader, Bethel Church
Redding, California
Author of *Born for Significance* and *The Way of Life*

For several years, Ken Williams and I have been watching an international drama unfold as God reveals Himself to people who experience same-sex attraction and gender confusion. As the CHANGED Movement began to take shape in 2018, hundreds of new friends from across the world began contacting us. We became aware that an unusual revival had begun. Other organizations like ours, which focus on sharing stories of God's love, had also sprung up on all the major continents. At the same time, as if in direct response, legislation has prevailed that blocks religious liberty for those seeking alternatives to the LGBTQ experience. Professional counseling and faith-based care is being restricted worldwide for anyone seeking change. At this timely and risky moment, Ken's book is a witness to our generation of how God touches the lives of those who seek Him wholeheartedly. In a time when culture wants to cancel our existence, his story and the insights God has given will be a lifeline.

Pastor Elizabeth Woning, MATS
Co-founder, CHANGED Movement and Equipped to Love

Ken Williams has done a masterful job of opening a wide door into the heart of God, a doorway that people identifying as both gay and straight can journey through with safety and hope. His book is at the same time disarming and intense. He doesn't dodge any difficult issues as he navigates his way out of darkness into the light and hope of Jesus. If you or a loved one struggle with sexual identity, you will be overwhelmed by the compassion of the Holy Spirit as you read.

Dr. Dan Carroll
Senior Pastor, Water of Life Community Church
Fontana, CA
Author of *Into the Heart of God*

More than three decades ago, I made a decision to reject my gay identity and walk a different path. What I wouldn't have given to have had this book as a guide! In it, Ken uses his own fascinating story to show someone what to expect when they say, as he did, "Now what, Lord?" It also serves as a terrific tool for pastors and ministry leaders who want to serve people wrestling with their own sexuality. Beautiful story, beautifully written.

Joe Dallas
Counselor and author of *Desires in Conflict*

Ken Williams' inspirational and brutally honest story describes how God's grace is powerful enough to overcome any obstacle. Those struggling with same-sex attraction, or those with loved ones who are, will be encouraged to know that change and transformation are possible through the gospel. The world says people like Ken do not exist. His testimony shouts back that all things are possible in Jesus.

Michael L. Brown, Ph.D.
Host of the Line of Fire broadcast
Author of *Can You Be Gay and Christian?*

Our world is grasping for answers to understand sexuality, especially as it pertains to the LGBTQ community. In *The Journey OUT*, Ken Williams unpacks the events of his own life, revealing God's heart to address sexual confusion. You will be drawn into the humanity of the story and walk away with a deeper sense of understanding about what God is doing on the earth in this community. Hidden in the events of his journey are practical steps that lead to freedom. More importantly than the contents of this book are the contents of his life; as a father of four, amazing husband, and great friend, Ken Williams is walking proof of the living gospel.

Caitlin and Cole Zick
Directors, Moral Revolution
Author (Caitlin) of Look at You, Girl

For the past 16 years we have witnessed Ken's God-given anointing to demonstrate grace for people in their weaknesses while diligently encouraging them toward the Lord. In *The Journey OUT*, Ken paints a picture of God's grace and power to bring lasting change into areas that some deem unchangeable. We believe that through this book, many will understand the value for helping the precious LGBTQ community out of their lifestyle when they request it.

Lori and Barry Byrne, LMFT
Co-founders, Nothing Hidden Ministries
Authors of Love After Marriage

What you're about to read is a story of our friend Ken who decided to be incredibly vulnerable about his own journey regarding his sexuality and same-sex attraction. We have watched what once was a struggle now become a beacon of light in a world that redefines what sexuality is in every aspect. His story proves that when Jesus promises He will save you, He will save every part of you. This book may be one of the most important books of our day as it addresses the issue of sexuality with the power of Jesus to those who are looking for truth.

Eric and Candace Johnson
Senior Pastors, Bethel Church
Redding, CA
Author (Eric) of Momentum

Ken Williams is a real gift to the global church of Jesus Christ. His potent insights about breaking shame and authentic sharing on the concept of surrender in *The Journey OUT* are powerful paradigm shifts for every Christian. This book is a helpful read for everyone who wants the church to be a safer community for people with same-sex attraction. I also highly recommend this for anyone who wants to come out and come home to the Father.

Ian Toh
Senior Pastor of 3:16 Church
Singapore
Co-Founder of TrueLove.Is Ministry

It would be easy to stand at a distance and put Ken Williams in some sort of protest category—a righter of wrongs, a critic of others' lifestyles, and a proponent of a God-inspired "right way" to live.

I know that some, perhaps many, will have done that, and perhaps more will along the way. What I want to say is that I know this man, and for as long as I have known him, he has had one overriding desire. That is, that all who come into contact with him or are influenced by him or the organizations which he serves become the best person that they can be in life and in their relationship with God and others.

The specific expression of this, related to this book, has been a work in progress, but it is completely in line with my experience of Ken. He wants you to be fully alive. His journey has been long, at times painful, but always aimed in the same direction. This book unpacks both of these themes, helping the reader with their journey and pointing them in the direction of being everything that they were created to be.

Ken's vulnerability is an invitation for you to be honest with yourself; his journey is a down payment for yours; and his outcome of discovering identity, intimacy with God, a family life, and hope for the future of fellow travelers is a prophetic light for all with eyes to see. A light which I have seen grow consistently brighter.

Ken has been my mentor, and then my employee, and finally my right-hand man in developing a ministry with global impact. All of those roles have been wonderful and productive in my life and in others, but it is Ken, the friend, the trusted confidant, the risk-taker with his own vulnerability, who I commend and endorse. You can trust Ken with your heart—after all, he has trusted his to you.

I encourage you, even before you read, to put Ken Williams in a category, a "box," as a type of person. That category, that "box," is simply this: Ken Williams cares deeply about people. It is a Christlike quality. His heart has found a voice, a target, and a modus operandi. His life, this book, and the companions who have gathered around him along the way are the evidence.

As you read, I believe that you will become a victim, not of pain or confusion, or of any other unacceptable experience, but of a man who has learned along his journey how loved he is and how much he wants you to experience the same.

Paul Manwaring
Member, Senior Leadership Team of Bethel Church
Redding, CA
Author of *What on Earth is Glory?* and *Things Fathers Do*

My first significant conversation with Ken Williams took place around a table at the birthday celebration of a mutual friend. Being a practiced observer, it didn't take long to recognize in Ken an authentic lover of

God with a passion to help hurting and misunderstood humanity. In *The Journey OUT*, he not only proves that to be true, but courageously lays his life down for the freedom of others.

David Crone
Senior Leader, The Mission
Vacaville, CA
Author of *Prisoner of Hope* and *Decisions that Define Us*

THE JOURNEY
OUT

KEN WILLIAMS

THE JOURNEY
OUT

HOW I FOLLOWED JESUS
AWAY FROM GAY

DESTINY IMAGE® PUBLISHERS, INC.
P.O. Box 310, Shippensburg, PA 17257-0310
"Promoting Inspired Lives."

This book and all other Destiny Image and Destiny Image Fiction books are available at Christian bookstores and distributors worldwide.

For more information on foreign distributors, call 717-532-3040.

Reach us on the Internet: www.destinyimage.com.

ISBN 13 TP: 978-0-7684-5581-6

ISBN 13 eBook: 978-0-7684-5582-3

ISBN 13 HC: 978-0-7684-5584-7

ISBN 13 LP: 978-0-7684-5583-0

For Worldwide Distribution, Printed in the U.S.A.

1 2 3 4 5 6 7 8 / 25 24 23 22 21

DEDICATION

This book is dedicated to all of you who are conflicted by unwanted same-sex desires or are disheartened by gender confusion. God cares about your pain and grief. While I don't know exactly what freedom is going to look like for you years from now, God did say that He would do exceedingly, abundantly above all we can ask or imagine. I know that the journey can be exhausting. Psalm 34:19 greatly encouraged me in my journey. It says, *"Many are the afflictions of the righteous, but the Lord delivers him out of them all."* I pray you experience God's strength and comfort as you journey toward wholeness in Him.

ACKNOWLEDGMENTS

Special thanks to my beautiful, gracious, and faithful wife, Tiffany. Your Christlike love and courage introduced me to a life I never dreamed of. This book would not exist without you.

And to these pastors and ministers who invited me in and created such safe spaces for me [in alphabetical order]: Mark and Rena Brookes, Barry and Lori Byrne, Hugh and Craig Cunningham, Ken and Donna Davies, Steve and Dawna De Silva, Bill and Krystal Grubbs, Barry and Margo Harwell, Eric and Sadie Hess, Bill and Beni Johnson, Ray Leight, Banning and SeaJay Liebscher, Paul and Sue Manwaring, Terry and Susan Moore, Mike and Celia Orand, Gary and Jennifer Paltridge, Bob and Claudia Perry, Mark Peterson, Jim and Heidi Roles, Dave and Karen Runyan, Danny and Sheri Silk, Randy and Tammy Skinner, John and Jill Stacher, Steve and Judy Swift, Kris and Kathy Vallotton, Roland and Shirin Worton, my Moral Revolution team, all the leadership of Sojourn Church and Bethel Church, and so many more!

And to my mom and dad, Judy and Waymon Williams: Your sacrificial love for me goes beyond anything reasonable. So many who share their homosexual feelings with their parents are met with cold religion or a welcome party into an alt-world, and neither are equipped to meet their needs. But I hit the jackpot. You drew closer and made my struggle your own. Mom, thanks for being the best listener on Earth and helping make this book possible. Dad, I miss you every day and am so grateful for how you graciously loved me when I was a confused young man.

And to my ministry partner, Elizabeth Woning: Your faith, compassionate heart, wisdom, and intimacy with God are all a huge gift to the world. I have been a regular recipient of these. I can't imagine having traveled this road without you. Thank you for your partnership, your friendship, and your contributions to this book.

And to my Equipped to Love and CHANGED families: You're a gift to me and to the world. My constant inspiration. Everything meaningful we've done bears your fingerprints! I am cheering for you all!

And to Abigail McKoy: Thank you for all your brilliant input, sensitive heart, bright ideas, and immense support!

DISCLAIMER

This book is not a formula or a magic wand. My intent is that it serves as a springboard to a deep life in God. All our hopes for transformation are found in our personal relationships with Jesus. Also, for the sake of protecting the identities of two individuals, I have changed some details in two instances of my personal story.

"Taste and see that the Lord is good...."

—Psalm 34:8

CONTENTS

Foreword 23

Preface 25

Introduction 27

Chapter 1   Different from the Other Boys 29

Chapter 2   Intimacy Breakdown 51

Chapter 3   Change Is Possible 65

Chapter 4   Vulnerability 81

Chapter 5   Surrender 97

Chapter 6   Relationships 113

Chapter 7   Identity 131

Chapter 8   Enduring Faith 147

Chapter 9   Vision 161

Chapter 10   The Fruit of the Battle 175

Chapter 11   Creating a Healing Environment 189

Frequently Asked Questions 203

Recommended Resources 223

About Ken Williams 231

FOREWORD

We are currently living in an era of time where a false narrative created by the political spirit is attempting to strip our children of their Godlikeness (Genesis 1:27). Gender and sexuality are now perceived to be fluid; masculinity has been confused, abandoned, and even villainized; young boys are unable to mature into true manhood; and young girls are left without protectors who provide and promote them into their God-given destinies. We are witnessing the effects of what I describe as the fatherless generation.

Contrary to popular opinion, the world is desperate to know that there is a reason to embrace your divine design (chromosomal sex and sexual orientation) instead of rejecting it. This is the powerfully anointed message that Ken Williams pens in his new book, *The Journey OUT*.

With open-hearted sincerity and beaming courage, Ken exposes to us what it's like to live in the skin of someone who battles with homosexuality. He candidly shares the innermost thoughts of his profoundly personal journey through sexual sin, giving us a vantage point to see what many within the Church refuse to acknowledge. This timely and story-driven book obliterates the political spirit's agenda and prophetically proclaims throughout its pages that *change is possible!*

Like my trusted friend Ken, I'm convinced that there is not one person on the face of the planet whom God has not made a way for! *The Journey OUT* brilliantly reminds us of that and creates moments with God where we are enveloped with His goodness and exposed to His ways; shame will have no hold over your heart or mind after exploring the well-written words, startling questions, and catalytic activations found within this book!

It's important to remember that over the course of our lives, we will have many mentors (either directly or indirectly) who will teach us essential life lessons; this is the hallmark of fatherhood. Ken Williams, refusing to turn his back on the fatherless generation, has dedicated his life to one of the most divisive topics among believers—sexuality. I believe that through his own testimony, Ken will father thousands of people into freedom and wholeness.

As Ken profoundly says in his book, "*We may have abdicated our position of authority in this arena because of fear and desire for control, but Jesus has called us to do more. Only followers of Jesus can say to someone with full confidence, 'There is hope.'*" Whether you're questioning your sexuality, a parent of a child who is battling with sexual sin, or a leader who refuses to turn their back on a generation desperate for fathers and mothers, may you find hope and courage in these pages!

Kris Vallotton
Leader, Bethel Church
Redding, CA
Co-Founder, Bethel School of Supernatural Ministry
Author of thirteen books, including *The Supernatural Ways of Royalty,*
Spirit Wars, and *Heavy Rain*

PREFACE

Homosexuality is a profoundly personal issue for people. Some have lost spouses or children to extramarital affairs, sexually transmitted infections, transgenderism, or suicide. Others have a current struggle themselves with unwanted same-sex desires. And still others could feel wounded or misunderstood merely by my stating that homosexuality is a path I chose not to travel.

However, I write this book because the world needs to know that Jesus paid for this area of pain. There is no grief or torment that His death on the cross and resurrection did not vanquish. I found my transformation out of homosexuality via the Church, so I have conviction that she can be the hands and feet of Jesus to those experiencing heartache over a confused sexual identity. It didn't happen for me overnight, but God set me free from porn, masturbation, and overwhelming sexual attraction to males and gave me sexual desire for my wife.

My intent is that this book will catalyze your connection with God, arm you with hope, and point you to any deep places where Jesus is desiring to meet you with love, grace, empowerment, or healing.

God has no ulterior motives. It was for freedom that He set you and me free.

INTRODUCTION

I remember so well the fear I had as a teenager that I would never be sexually aroused by a woman or have a successful marriage to a wife. It seemed that nobody would ever be able to relate to my humiliating struggle, let alone offer me real help. This book is the fulfillment of a 20-year dream that I would one day be able to offer to others the encouragement I had to fight so many years to find.

I know many people who have left LGBTQ behind, and what is clear is that Jesus has been at work in similar areas in each of our lives—healing our emotional wounds, replacing lies we'd believed with truth, drawing us close to Himself, and helping us build life-giving relationships.

The kinds of freedom I've experienced came as a result of leaning wholeheartedly upon God and the promises in His Word—by selling out to Him and holding nothing back. In this book, I highlight the primary areas of spiritual life where I've seen the Lord meet people struggling with their sexual identity. And I offer the same counsel that resulted in breakthrough for me and my friends.

Whether you are seeking wholeness and freedom for yourself or for a loved one, this book can help you. I encourage you not to just absorb the information but to invite the Lord to lead you on your own intimacy journey. In Him, we find everything that we need.

Chapter 1

DIFFERENT FROM
THE OTHER BOYS

I sat down on the couch and turned on the TV. I had just put the two-year-old I was babysitting to bed, and his parents wouldn't be home for a little while. Flipping through the channels, I landed on a Lifetime movie and settled in to relax. As I watched the narrative unfold, though, the movie began to grip me. A mixture of dread and profound curiosity flooded my body.

I watched the life of a young man who was loved by his family, active in his community, and seemingly happy. Something felt a little off as he tried to fit in with his male friends, but he appeared to be fairly content. Soon, though, the story revealed how miserable he truly was. Hiding from his father, the main character anxiously disclosed to his mother his secret shame: He was sexually attracted to other men.

Suddenly, it became clear that all of those interactions with other guys during the early scenes of the film had been an elaborate performance. He had been trying to assimilate into a male culture through athletics, creating a fictional sexual history with women so he could fit in with the other guys. But as he explained dramatically to his mother, living a lie had become too much for him. He tearfully told her, "I'm gay. It's true and it just keeps getting truer." Although he hadn't had any sexual encounters with men, he explained that he could just feel it. Inner turmoil evident on his face, he confessed how confused and lost he felt. Hiding her own emotions, his mom confidently assured him that they were going to get him help; they would fix this together.

I was stunned. I stayed glued to the movie, eager to see how in the world this guy was going to get any help for his same-sex attraction and escape from his obvious anguish. It was more than just an engaging plotline, though. This movie was telling my story. The main character was putting into words exactly how I felt—I, too, was different from the other boys. His shame and inner turmoil were the same as my own. This was the first moment in my life I felt like I could fully relate to someone, like I wasn't all alone in my pain and confusion, and that guy was gay. My life was unfolding on the screen in front of me. I was horrified.

Growing Up Scrawny

Growing up, I was the scrawniest kid in every one of my classes. To make matters worse, I seemed to have emerged from the womb with a pastoral gifting, preferring deep conversation and heart-to-heart connection over most of the stereotypically masculine activities. My dad really loved me and enjoyed being with me, my mom, and my sister. But for various reasons we had difficulty connecting emotionally. He loved Jesus but didn't express his faith in God in the same ways that I did; he tended to avoid thinking about sad things while I delighted in exploring the depths of the heart, and his work kept him away from home a fair amount while I was growing up.

My dad could see, early on, that I didn't feel confident in myself or in my relationships with other boys. So he did what he knew how to do—he enrolled me in karate, then soccer, then baseball, then Boy Scouts. He came to most of my games, meets, and campouts, cheering me on and encouraging me the whole time. I knew that he loved me, but it didn't change the fact that I wasn't thriving in those activities. There were no joyous memories of taking home-run victory laps, waving to my proud father in the stands. I struggled. I warmed the bench, each time receiving the disappointing reminder that I wasn't quite up to the challenge of masculinity. He was usually with me at these sporting events, encouraging his unhappy athlete, but I almost never left feeling successful or like our connection had grown.

My dad wasn't some stereotypically gruff man; he was actually unusually kind and gentle. But he looked pretty masculine, and he loved hunting, fishing, and camping. I was his scrawny son who couldn't care less about football and was allergic to the outdoors. I loved talking to people, learning about their deep thoughts and feelings. And I had a hunger for spiritual growth. I had had a profound salvation experience at eight years old, and my love for God was deep. I was looking for spiritual role models, but I didn't see any men in my community or church who, from my perspective, were passionately pursuing God.

I did, however, see women who wanted to speak about their faith and talk deeply with one another. The men I observed at church seemed to want to keep conversations superficial and centered around sports. So I found myself talking to my mom and her friends, sometimes for hours. At school, I gravitated to the girls my age. They didn't care as much about my height or athletic prowess. With them, I could be the funny guy or the smart one, always ready with a witty quip or side comment. I wasn't winning any hearts, but I wasn't getting rejected either.

Name Calling

None of these attributes improved my standing with the other boys. For all of my differences, I was teased mercilessly. As the young men around me began to flex their proverbial muscles, exploring their masculinity in a social setting, I became more and more alienated from them. Walking home from elementary school, the mocking names were cruel and humiliating. Some boys would yell, "Hey, Gay Wad!" or "Hey, Shrimp!" or "Hey, Faggot!" It wasn't just some physical attribute of mine—skinny legs or a funny haircut—that was being mocked; it was my very identity as a male. I began to receive the message that I was less than, that I wasn't adequate as a young man, that I was someone who wanted to have sex with other men. All I wanted to do was hide, avoiding other guys whenever possible. I knew I wasn't a girl, but I also was becoming very aware that I wasn't like the other boys. They had made that very clear.

As I grew up, my experiences with sexuality were confusing at best. At eight years old, a male babysitter opened up the centerfold of a pornographic magazine, showing me the photo of the naked woman inside. "Doesn't that turn you on?" he asked. *Apparently it **doesn't** turn me on,* I thought, *whatever that means. What does that say about me?*

I was eight. I didn't know why I wasn't having the reaction to the nude photo that he expected. All I really understood was that, in the eyes of this cool, older guy, I had somehow failed an unspoken test of masculinity.

At another kid's house, some friends and I found pornographic magazines underneath their parents' bed. Under one side were stacks of *Playgirl* and, under the other side, *Playboy*. We pulled them out, curious about the content, looking at the photos inside. When I started looking at the *Playgirl* displaying photos of naked men, a girl in our group took notice. "Oh," she said, "so you like to look at the men, huh?" I was looking at both, as were all of the kids, but the implication pierced my heart. I thought to myself, *Why **was** I looking at that magazine? What if something is wrong with me?*

Not long after that, I was playing in a nearby field with some friends. One of the other kids found a box hidden in the grass. Opening it up, we found stacks of hardcore gay pornography. I saw men urinating onto each other and having oral and anal sex with each other. I didn't know those actions were in the realm of human experience. It confused me about men, my own body, and even the very world in which I lived. Walking away, I literally felt damaged. After that, one of the boys initiated some naked play and inappropriate touching with me. For the months following, whenever I would return to my friend's house, I felt intrigued by the sexualized world that might again open up there. I remember becoming routinely sexually aroused upon arriving at that house. Something had been awakened in me that I couldn't explain. I felt so dirty.

At eight or nine years old, I overheard a respected friend of our family talking about sex. She wished God hadn't even created sex because it just complicated things. She suggested we'd be better off without it because it created a whole lot of problems. I took that information in until I formed a few conclusions: Sex was for people who were less godly, and so, in order to not be one of them, I would just never have sex; I would opt out entirely—an easy decision to make when you haven't yet experienced a sex drive.

Judgment Cycle

By age ten, I had subconsciously made a ruling on masculinity: Men were less than. They weren't as spiritual, they weren't as capable, they couldn't even handle a deep conversation, they were obtuse and unfeeling, and they were less godly than women. Men were inferior and, I decided, sex was bad. Jesus hadn't had sex. Paul wrote that it was better to remain celibate if you could control yourself. But without being aware of it, I made an inner vow: I wasn't going to be like other men. I was going to be better than them. I was going to be like God. And I set out to do so all on my own.

The Bible says, *"Do not judge, or you too will be judged. For in the same way you judge others, you will be judged, and with the measure you use, it will be measured to you"* (Matthew 7:1-2 NIV). In hindsight, it is clear to me that this biblical principle was at work in my life and predisposed me to experiencing same-sex attraction. Because I did not feel comfortable with or safe around males, I judged them. It was how I protected myself. Judging them seemingly gave me permission to do masculinity differently—my way. But the more I judged other males, the more disconnection and distance I felt from them. Judgment was being measured back to me.

I did the same thing with the whole concept of having sex. From what I'd seen, it looked animalistic, barbaric, and ungodly and, therefore, hard to envision for my own life. It seemed much easier to judge sex as beneath me, so I judged it—just like I judged masculinity. But this arrogance, or judgment of God's designs for identity and procreation, left me feeling even more isolated. I relied almost completely on my intellect and humor to navigate social situations with my peers at school and to feel connected to and known by other people. Eventually,

I completely opted out of masculinity. I decided to merely be "a person" as opposed to being a male. It was my way of avoiding all of the pressure and trying to survive.

Despite these efforts to peacefully navigate my life, I felt broken, confused, and lonely. My male peers increasingly rejected me, and the world around me seemed to only accommodate people who presented themselves as either distinctly masculine or distinctly feminine. Society had certain expectations of me as a male. I felt the weight of those throughout my day—entering the boys' locker room, attending the seventh grade dance, going to gym class, witnessing a group of girls being disrespected by a boy. Even buying a pack of gum from a male cashier seemed to confront me with expectations about my role as a male. Was I standing properly? Did my speech sound effeminate? Could he tell that I didn't measure up as a male? From my perspective, I disappointed every time.

In my head, the real me was so detestable that I couldn't let anyone fully see me. And so, it felt like no one truly knew me. I was lonely to my very core.

Enter, stage right: masturbation! In my early teens, I accidentally discovered this incredible tool for briefly numbing all of my pain. For a few moments, I would feel relief from the constant inner turmoil. But just as quickly as the relief came, it would leave. And I was left in my pain. So, I began to use masturbation every day, multiple times a day. In hindsight, I can see that it was a coping mechanism, but in the moment all I could feel was guilt and shame. Despite this, my addiction raged on, and, even though I attempted to quit countless times, I was never able to do so.

As I got older, my detachment from other males left a vacuum of masculinity in my life. I had pushed men away, and they had pushed me away. I had moved further and further away from men and closer to women, who didn't seem to expect me to be different from who I was. Femininity felt most comfortable and familiar. But masculinity became exotic and foreign, and soon I was craving it. Let me explain.

Beginning in first grade, I developed a series of emotionally dependent, and sometimes codependent, relationships with other males. Codependency is understood to be "a psychological condition or a relationship in which a person manifesting low self-esteem and a strong desire for approval has an unhealthy attachment to another person and places the needs of that person before his or her own."[1] In its most extreme form, it's hard for an individual to even see where he/she starts and the other person ends. These were not sexual relationships for me, but rather evidence that I was just starving for masculinity, for connection to it. So I would find the most popular, strongest, most self-assured guy and, in my desire to be what he was, I would attach myself to him. I couldn't find that kind of masculinity within myself, so I needed to discover it externally.

But not once did I ever think, "I guess I should be gay." That never crossed my mind as an option. I went to school in the '80s. I don't think I knew one gay person. I doubt anyone I knew, at that time, would have known anyone who identified as gay. So as I sat on that couch, watching that Lifetime movie unfold, it felt as if a horrifying puzzle was suddenly coming together for me. As I mentioned earlier in my story, this main character, a boy about my age who had experienced all of the same rejection, pain, and the confusing pull toward men, declared that he was a homosexual. I was glued to the screen when he first met with a psychiatrist desiring resolution of his unwanted same-sex attraction. I watched as he told his family and as his relationship with his father unraveled. And then, with a sinking despair, I understood that he wasn't going to receive the help he was looking for. There was nothing the psychiatrist could do. The message of the film, instead, was, "This is just how you were made. Everyone needs to adjust and get used to it."

But this was the 1980s. Gay was not OK; it wasn't chic. To be gay meant that there was a scarlet letter tacked to your shirt. But suddenly, as I watched my life replicated on the screen, I believed that I was gay. The first moment in my life that I felt like someone else could totally relate to me—to my rejection, humiliation, and confusion—was the same moment I was realizing my identity was something totally forbidden and undesired by me. He was gay, and I was gay. I was flooded with hopelessness and an all-consuming panic.

Connecting completely with the character in the film, I spiraled into despair. I didn't want to be gay! It wasn't a life I felt that God condoned or had planned for me. I had no desire to be involved in a sexual relationship with a man. I'd been raised in the church and had given my life to Jesus. I hadn't encountered Him fully yet, but I had genuine faith and a desire to please God and live righteously. There was no one in my world talking about freedom or redemption at that time. The only message I'd heard from the church was that homosexuals were awful, they were sinners, and they were definitely going to hell. My understanding was that people with same-sex attraction represented the worst possible version of humanity and, if Christians were being really honest, it would be a whole lot better for everyone if they weren't even around.

"Thorn in My Flesh," They Said

I knew that a life of gay sex was not what I wanted, but my infatuations with other guys and my same-sex attraction continued. Along the

37

way, one of them turned sexual. One night, I was having a sleepover with a guy friend who had become my most recent fixation. That particular night, we were sharing a bed and, without warning, he stuck his hand down my pants.

This was not an advance I would have made myself because of my deep convictions about sexual sin, but I was so emotionally needy that a part of me was thrilled. My own need for affirmation was so great that, when he touched me, my first thought was, *A guy values me enough to touch me. I'm being pursued here...by this impressive guy.* After years of feeling inadequate and repulsive, his affection and validation seemed impossible to refuse. Plus, it felt good.

For months, we engaged in sessions of mutual masturbation. A part of me felt elated that someone wanted to be close to me. Here was a guy I liked and admired who wasn't ashamed of me. He actually wanted to touch me and be with me. But at the same time, I was being eaten alive by guilt. I knew very well what the Bible had to say about homosexuality and fornication. But the desire for affection from a real, impressive male overwhelmed my fear of punishment. I worked hard to not allow myself to think about what God might be thinking of my sinful sexual behavior because I had no solution. All I knew was that a bigger, stronger, attractive guy appreciated me, saw me, and pursued me. I knew this wasn't the life that God meant for me, but I seemed powerless to extricate myself from the recurring sexual encounters, which were always immediately followed by deep shame. Thankfully, we moved away and the relationship ended. The repetitive cycle was broken, but so was my source of affirmation and identity.

Fast-forward several years, and my experience of same-sex attraction felt overwhelming. The feelings of hopelessness and shame had only grown. Not knowing anywhere else to turn, I finally went to the Christian bookstore wearing a disguise. I was horrified at the thought of anyone being witness to my struggle and, in the pre-internet world, there was no way to search for resources in the privacy of your own home. So, I pulled my ball cap down over my face and walked inside. Ducking around the aisles, I tried to find some help for myself. There wasn't a single book about homosexuality anywhere on the shelves.

Finally, inside of a larger, "all of the things that could possibly be wrong with you" type of book, I found a half-page entry on the subject of homosexuality. In matter-of-fact language, it let me know that if I was dealing with same-sex attraction, I should consider it to be my "thorn in the flesh." It continued with something like, "God has given this to you to deal with for the rest of your life. You are responsible, though, to rise above the temptation and never act out on your sexual feelings. You're just going to have to white-knuckle it. So, good luck. But to help you in this journey, you'll need to develop a lifelong relationship with a Christian counselor. This will end up costing you somewhere around $250,000."

I was 17 years old, making $3.35 an hour as a busboy. I didn't have a quarter of a million dollars to work on personal development! I'd walked into the Christian bookstore, hopeful that I could find godly wisdom to help me overcome my struggle with homosexuality. But instead, all I found was irredeemable advice, recommendations of more self-reliance and self-effort. God wouldn't be coming through for me. I walked out suicidal.

I was so isolated from other males in high school that I was craving attention and connection. I had developed a new codependency, this time focused on my youth pastor. He was athletic, a few years older, and passionate in his pursuit of the Lord. A real evangelist. I admired his God-oriented life so much. So I became the most dedicated young man in his youth group. My desire to be spiritual was genuine, and he responded to my earnest passion for God with affirmation, attention, and spiritual guidance. I lapped it up, desperate to fill the deficits in my heart.

It didn't bother me a bit that he was married or that he had no idea the weight I put on his presence. By the end of high school, I was experiencing near constant emotional turmoil. I was so desperate and so alone in my struggle that I felt like I was losing my ability to deal with reality. I felt completely out of control, and I stopped being able to see a future for myself. There was such an emotional battle going on within me that I felt like I was unraveling. And the only time I felt OK was in the pastor's presence and, ideally, when I was receiving direct attention from him. I became entirely dependent on him for my mental and emotional well-being. If I hadn't received enough attention, I would pursue it myself. At the height of my obsession, I would drive half an hour across town to sit in my car outside of his house just so I could feel like I was a little closer to him. But obviously no meaningful connection happens by sitting alone outside someone's home, so before long I started trying to find other ways to get his attention. I lived a daily fantasy of receiving affirmation from this guy, and I don't think he had any idea.

Coming Clean

In my desperation to find relief, I began considering ways I could end my life. It's not that I wanted to kill myself. I just didn't want to live any longer. Life was too hard. So, I imagined ways to end my life that wouldn't have technically been my fault. Like, what if my car just didn't stop fast enough at an intersection and drifted into cross-traffic? That way my family wouldn't have to live with a suicide on their consciences. But then I realized that I didn't want the car wreck to hurt anyone else, either. I didn't know what to do. So in an effort to find any relief from the war in my mind, I, an honor-roll student, began skipping school and letting my grades slide. I wanted to do anything I could to minimize the pressure and expectations on my life.

A few weeks after finding no hope in the bookstore, it all became just too much for me to bear. I was terrified that there was something deeply wrong with me, and my inability to find any positive pathway forward had become more than I could handle alone. So, I went down into our basement and wrote out nine pages of hate, vulgarity, and pain. I skipped school the next day, showed up at my church unannounced, and handed over my desperate writing to my youth pastor. And as we sat in the car at the McDonald's drive-thru, he read it while I sat frozen in my seat. Finally, he looked up and casually stated, "Well, Ken. You're not gay."

I stared at him. *What?!* I thought, *How could anyone read that letter and arrive at that conclusion? What part of "I'm only sexually attracted to other men" don't you understand?*

"We are going to tell your parents," he added. And then I was terrified.

"Of all the things that we are gonna do today, that is *not* one of them," I said. But he insisted and—deep inside—I felt relief. I had wanted to tell them for years, but I was scared, scared of what they would think of me and scared to blow up my family. But finally, my parents would know. I wouldn't be so alone with the weight of this. I had no idea how they were going to react, though. I knew they loved me deeply, but we had been strongly influenced by some very strict, rules-focused ministers and churches. There was no grace theology in my understanding of God. My family had worked so hard to live righteously, and I knew that what I had to say was going to shock them. But finally, I had no choice. It was out now, and my pastor had taken over the reins of communication.

When the day came to talk to my mom and dad, I was a nervous wreck. My sister was only 13 years old at the time, so I asked her to stay in her room because I had something very painful to tell our parents. "Don't come out," I pleaded with her, "no matter what you hear." My youth pastor finally arrived, and the four of us took a seat around our breakfast table. He initiated the conversation for me, and then I poured out my heart to them. Years of pain and confusion spilled out as I explained the hidden, inner struggle, the sexual sin, and the hopelessness that dominated me. For hours, we sat around that table and talked together. I'll never forget seeing my mother and father weep over my pain. There was no anger, only sadness and concern about the fear and trauma I'd been carrying.

Finally, my dad asked, "What do you want, Ken? Do you want to live that kind of life?"

"No," I said, "I've never wanted to live a gay life."

"OK, then we're going to get you some help." And, just like that, I could breathe. There was now at least a chance that my future might be livable.

Finally, I didn't have to carry the weight of my worries and emotional pain on my own. My parents were on my team. I was going to get help. From that moment on, I began to talk deeply with my mom and increasingly with my dad as well. I shared with them, finally, the depth of my struggles and pain. It felt so good to not have to deal with everything all on my own. In one evening, I was released from solitary confinement and set free on a long path of transformation. However disruptive it was to my family's life, it also cracked open a need for deeper emotional and relational healing in all of us. My family changed. Whereas before we didn't often talk about deep, emotional things, now we didn't shy away from the tough subjects. My pursuit of resolution for my sexual identity issues catalyzed my family into realizing things about their own emotional states that had been previously ignored. A revolution began in my family, and I felt hope for the first time.

Wait, God Is Good?

I began meeting with a Christian counselor regularly, slowly laying the foundation of transformation as I went off to college. I wasn't yet free from my same-sex urges or sexual attractions, but the possibility of getting free felt enticing on its own.

At a college party, seeking to embrace (my misapplication of) God's grace, I chugged five beers in 20 minutes and proceeded to pass out. In the morning, still reeling from the night before, I began to experience a type of acidic stomach regurgitation that I'd never felt before. I had constant heartburn and even some damage to my esophagus. It was horrible, night and day, and it wouldn't go away. I downed antacid, got prescription drugs, and spent thousands of dollars of my parents' money on gastroenterologists and at holistic wellness clinics. But after five years of nonstop pain, no one could tell me what was wrong. After an allergy test revealed that I was allergic to almost every major food, eating became an expensive and elusive challenge. My diet consisted of pork, asparagus, and other rare protein sources, like buffalo. In spite of adhering to this crazy new diet, I was still miserable, and I was too sick to hold down a job.

Grasping at straws, I agreed to an experimental test at a wellness clinic to see if a hernia was causing my pain. I was supposed to receive a few drops of hydrochloric acid down my esophagus. Instead, an oblivious intern injected me with an entire large syringe of acid. I immediately passed out. They revived me with oxygen and sent me home with narcotics to numb the pain. For weeks, I was only occasionally conscious as they tried flushing my stomach so that I could keep down any sort of food. I'd wake up, try to eat something, throw up, and then pass out again. I was in bad shape, and I wasn't getting any better.

One day, a former college roommate, Brian Kelly, called me out of the blue. He told me that he was attending Kenneth Hagin's Bible school, Rhema, and he'd just wanted to check in on me. I told him about my health struggles and he said something shocking: "Dude, God doesn't want you to be sick."

"I'm sorry, what?" I had been raised with the understanding that everything that happened on the earth was the will of God. I let him know that I'd never heard anything like that, and I'd been in church my whole life, thank you very much.

He responded, "Well, you've been going to the wrong churches." My curiosity was piqued. It was a nice thought that God didn't want me to suffer in this way, but it seemed too good to be true. At that point, though, my life was dominated by pain and sickness, so, when Brian offered to pray for my healing, I thought, *What do I have to lose?*

We decided to meet halfway, at my parents' home in Oklahoma. After almost getting stranded in a freak ice storm, I finally made it. My dad was out of town, but my mom was there and my sister had driven up from Waco, Texas to be with me. Brian had said that he wouldn't pray for me until I believed that God wanted to heal me. I think he understood that he had his work cut out for him, because he started to tell us testimonies to help build our faith.

Brian shared testimony after testimony of miraculous healing stories from his time at Rhema Bible School. And my mom, sister, and I would then ask questions. "If God still heals people physically supernaturally today, why don't I hear those stories on CNN? And, why am I just now hearing about this? Isn't this too good to be true?"

This went on for a day and a half. Just after midnight on February 4, 1996, Brian and I were sitting on the couch watching a Christian news broadcast called the 700 Club, and I asked to look at the list of healing Scriptures he had shown me. So, he handed me four pages compiled by minister Keith Moore, which he had received from his school: 101 Scriptures on healing. I began to read through them. *Is physical healing truly biblical and applicable to me today?* I wondered.

I read Isaiah 53:4, *"Surely our griefs He Himself bore, and our sorrows He carried"* (NASB). The verse note said that "griefs" could also be translated as "sickness," and it included a reference to Matthew 8. So I turned there. I read about Jesus healing everyone who was ill and then immediately following, in verse 17, I read, *"This was to fulfill what was spoken through Isaiah the prophet: 'He Himself took our infirmities and carried away our diseases.'"* Something clicked, and a smile spread across my face. Jesus was making a point of saying that physical healing is included in His atonement, which Isaiah had prophesied was coming. Jesus' sacrificial death on the cross had not only paid for all my sins but had also provided for my physical healing! And because the power of the atonement is available to everyone, I realized, His healing was available to me!

I looked up at Brian, grinning, "I think I believe that God wants to heal me."

Brian went and got my mom and sister, and they all laid hands on me. He prayed and commanded a spirit of infirmity to leave me. As soon as he'd said that, my stomach started churning, growling loudly, and I could feel things physically changing. At one point, I felt what I can only describe as a spirit of chaos being pulled out of my entire body, even from my fingertips and then collecting along my spine. Then, as if my story wasn't weird enough, God added the element of surprise. The farting started.

For much of the next five hours, I farted. And farted. If Guinness tracked such things, they'd have remotely detected the gas and given me a call. Hilariously, this was such evidence of a miracle that, every time I farted, my mother would lift her hands and say, "Praise the Lord!" My body had been bloated for five years and, with each passing of gas, I felt like whatever illness had been in me was draining away like water from a stopped sink. All four of us stayed up throughout the night, worshiping God from the pages of our Baptist hymnal. At some point, I felt hungry, so my mom made me a baked potato piled high with all kinds of foods I wasn't supposed to eat. I swallowed it easily and, for the first time in five years, I was able to eat without any pain or nausea.

When I woke up the next morning, the pain was all back and, this time, it was even worse. Totally discouraged, I wanted to be left alone, but Brian was adamant, "That's a spirit, Ken. You command it to leave you right now. Say it out loud." I did, and the pain left. And then 30 seconds later, it returned. So, I did it again and again, fighting for over a month for my complete healing. But during that time, the Lord was discipling me about building my faith, standing on His Word, and maintaining the supernatural healing He had given me. From that point on, my spiritual life exploded. I began to experience God in new ways and feel closer to Him than I ever had. I was free from all medication and no longer suffered any issues with my stomach or digestive system.

And something else had been deposited in me through that miracle—suddenly, I knew from my own experience that God was good, that He was loving, and that He wanted me to be healed. Even though I had brought on the severe illness through my own binge drinking, He had healed me. He'd pursued me with His love until I was totally free. I suddenly realized that, if He said homosexuality was wrong, then He must have a solution for that challenge as well! I began to anticipate His miraculous intervention in every area of my life.

I began to pursue all aspects of God, seeking out church services where they pursued supernatural healing and manifestations of the power of the Holy Spirit. In that journey, I began to see more and more of God's power and concern for my life and, through that, I realized that there could be some demonic element to my identity issues. I knew I had pain and rejection to work through, but I wondered whether a demonic spirit could be influencing me. I started to pursue deliverance ministry and—sure enough—I realized that some of what I'd been experiencing was the enemy's influence, causing me to believe lies about myself. I came out of one deliverance session free from the weight of some of those lies and, literally, measured half an inch taller. Fits of anger that I had dealt with since I was a child suddenly and completely left.

At one point, I had a middle-of-the-night, sobering encounter with a demon in my bedroom. I saw a misshapen heart standing beside my bed. But this wasn't a depiction of a happy heart. This heart was dark and slimy—grotesque. I realized that God was showing me a spirit of perversion. It was as if I had seen the pathetic, unappealing man pulling the levers behind the curtain. This creature was disgusting. It was empowering to realize that my battle wasn't just a personal one; it was

: as well. I began to pursue the presence of God above
and, incrementally, I began to experience my sexuality

I wish I could say that my challenges ended overnight, but that's
not how it happened. Battling the demonic was merely one element
of my struggle. And finding freedom was a progression. There were
ups and downs as I began to learn about my identity in Christ. In the
midst of multiple, powerful encounters with God, I also had moments
of confusion and deep loneliness. Trying to fill that void, I would occasionally go to adult bookstores to find gay porn that I could rent or
buy, sometimes binging for the entire weekend on the videos. I visited
an erotic massage parlor at one point. Another time, I wandered into a
porn theatre and participated in a sexual encounter in the dark with a
stranger. Every physically attractive male who crossed my path would
become sexualized in my mind. Even male characters on innocent TV
shows were not immune to my constant objectification. The hunger
felt insatiable sometimes, but God's grace was so much bigger.

I was on a journey, discovering who God is as Father, as Comforter,
and as Healer. I had incredible people walking beside me, mentoring
me. And I had the Holy Spirit partnering with me for my freedom. The
next few years were much more fruitful, and I slowly began to feel
more whole.

Rhinestones and Hair Twirls

During my three years at Bethel School of Supernatural Ministry
in Redding, California, homosexuality was losing its dominance in my
life. I started to notice that I wasn't objectifying men much anymore. I

stopped being hyper-aware of their body parts, and I wasn't as emotionally dependent upon one individual man. I had developed some great relationships with men who authentically accepted me, so my interactions came easier and were less fraught with tension and need. In the following chapters, I'll share more about what that journey looked like in this time frame.

In 2004, after completing the three years at BSSM, I returned to Dallas and became one of the leaders of my church's young adults. I started to consistently notice one of the girls who attended the group. I found myself unusually intrigued by her. At one of our evening gatherings, I caught myself looking at this girl and thinking, "Look at her wearing that sparkly belt. She's so cute!" I couldn't stop looking at her and noticing the way that she played with her hair. I thought, *I've never been enticed by what a girl was wearing or found it intriguing that she would be playing with her long hair.* Little things began to change for me. I began to really enjoy interacting with this girl. I loved being around her, I respected her, I started to notice how beautiful she was and, suddenly, I realized that I preferred to talk to her more than anyone else. I didn't just desire a friendship with her. I wanted to really *know* her. *Who is this beautiful creature?* I would catch myself thinking. These were all new experiences for me. So I did the only logical thing: I took her on a date!

That night, we went to a nice restaurant, and we sat down at a booth to order. As we started to look at the menu, though, she stood up to use the restroom. As she walked past me, she reached over and gently touched my shoulder. Electricity shot throughout my body. I was stunned. *Wow! That's good. I like that,* I thought. And so a couple hours later, I decided that, if she would have me, this was the woman I was going to marry. And ten months later, in August of 2006, I did just that.

Note

1. Merriam-Webster.com, s.v. "Codependency," accessed July 27, 2020, https://www.merriam-webster.com/dictionary/codependency.

Chapter 2

INTIMACY BREAKDOWN

For so many years, I lived in a fantasy world. Whichever boy I had fixated on as the object of my attention would become a consistent presence in my mind, an imaginary measuring stick of my own self-worth. In my classroom at school, I would hit the trash can with my wadded-up paper ball and dream about what a certain guy would say if he'd seen it. When I got a good grade, made a passable joke, or threw the frisbee well, I would daydream about the affirmation and attention this idolized boy might give me. My heart ate it up.

It took me many years to understand that my fixation on these other boys wasn't the problem in and of itself. My same-sex attraction wasn't even the real issue. I didn't have a "sexuality problem" as much as I had an intimacy problem. For me, intimacy is about feeling deeply known, uniquely valued, and unconditionally loved. It can include sexual intercourse but doesn't necessarily. I struggled to believe I belonged to God and that I belonged among my male peers. I had an intimacy problem. And though this seems obvious now, I was completely unaware of it at the time. I only realize in hindsight how atypical that behavior was—to be so regularly and intensely daydreaming of affirmation from certain male peers. And I certainly didn't see the root of my struggle until much later.

When we exhibit unwanted behavior in our lives, the temptation can be to begin to focus entirely on changing or stopping that behavior—controlling our actions through sheer willpower—instead of realizing that unhealthy behavior is the mask that unmet need wears. So if our behavior needs to change, we need to discover what need that behavior is attempting to meet. Shame isolates us, driving us deeper into self-hatred as we fail time and again to break the unhealthy cycles in our lives. Those of us who are struggling with same-sex attraction or confusion about our biological sex can begin to feel helpless as we see our determination to change collapse in the face of addiction and overwhelming need. We think our issues are all about sexual perversion, but that's often where we get it wrong.

We cannot point to one singular cause of same-sex attraction or sexual identity confusion. Each individual is unique, and what might deeply impact one person may not influence another in the same way. The wounds that can lead to challenges in one's sexuality are as wide and varied as the wounds that lead to other life issues.

I know that being short and scrawny and insecure invited mockery, and being called identity-challenging names by my young male peers gave me a negative perception of masculinity. And the challenges I then had connecting relationally with those guys and my difficulty bonding emotionally with my father hampered my ability to *see* myself as a male/a man. The porn I was shown did further damage, opening doors to the lying, accusational voice of the enemy, whereby shame, self-hatred, and lies about my identity became regulars in my thought life. And the inappropriate touching from my friend awakened parts of me that were not yet meant to be opened, directly sexualizing male-to-male connection—all before I was 10 years old. I've spoken to many others who report a history, obviously with different details, but with elements very similar to mine. Still others tell tragic stories of neglect, a parent who was impossible to please, or physical, emotional, or sexual abuse and how those events impacted their emotions and beliefs. But the common thread I see is that people's experiences of intimacy— their senses of love, value, and belonging—somewhere along the way were damaged.

This is significant because we were *made* for the interchange of intimacy; it is a deep need within us that never goes away! So, if we haven't learned to get it in healthy ways or if we've been damaged in our ability to do so, we just try to get that intimacy tank filled any way we know how. For me, it was through fantasy and emotional dependence. The true cry of my heart was for real intimacy. But I was never really receiving that because the wounded places inside me prevented me from receiving the healthy, safe love that was being offered to me. That legitimate need for intimacy was not getting met, and now I was also suffering because I was failing to control my own behavior. I was stuck on a hamster wheel, cycling between deep shame and deep hunger with seemingly no way out. God felt like a distant judge. I felt broken, fundamentally flawed, and consistently disappointed in my attempts to change myself.

Wired for Intimacy

There is a different way forward, though. Each one of us has been hardwired for intimacy. We long to be uniquely known and to feel deeply valued for who we are. It's no surprise that, if that need isn't met in the way that God intended, that longing could also manifest itself in our sexuality. Genesis says, "*Now Adam knew Eve his wife, and she conceived and bore Cain*" (Genesis 4:1). That word *knew* in Hebrew is *yada*, which means to comprehend or to discover, but it also means to know intimately in the covenant act of sexual intercourse between husband and wife. Sex is the most vulnerable and the deepest way that we can be known, so it makes sense that, if our ability to feel known and valued is disrupted, we may try to get those needs met in a sexual way. Especially if we've had an experience that opened a sexual door in the past. But those needs will never be fully satisfied by sexual activity. Our heart's cry for intimacy must be met, first and foremost, by our heavenly Father.

Instead of focusing on the challenges or insecurities we're facing with our sexual identities, we find transformation in our pursuit of intimacy with God. This shift can feel scary, especially for those of us who have been trying to white-knuckle our behavior into submission. But God wants to bring us into wholeness—which is emotional well-being and stability—so that we are no longer controlled by or compelled by same-sex sexual desires. I'll be referencing this idea of wholeness by saying "healing" or "freedom" in future sections of this book. Always the intended meaning will be living free from inner torment and compulsions; being at peace and knowing joy. For many of us, this journey into intimate connection with God led to changes in our sexual experiences.

Shifting the focus off of controlling our behavior can feel to some like a laissez faire, or even irresponsible, attitude toward harmful choices. But nothing could be further from the truth. Scripture says that we become what we behold (see 2 Corinthians 3:18). If our focus is constantly on our own failure and sin, we can become stuck in that way of thinking. However, when we shift our goal from "stop sinning" to a vision of walking intimately with God, our focus changes. We can begin to take the pressure off of ourselves to try to change our sexuality and, instead, begin to focus on our relationship with the One who created us, the only One who can bring real transformation to our lives.

Intimacy with God

The enemy would love nothing more than to convince us that a deep and genuine relationship with God isn't possible for us. He shows his hand throughout the Bible, trying to convince people that God isn't on their side, that they're too far gone for His mercy, that He's withholding good things from them, that He's abandoned them. These are lies straight from hell. The very foundation of creation is based on the truth that God wants to be with us. He wants to know and be known by us. Look at David. David is praised by God as "*a man after My own heart, who will do all My will*" (Acts 13:22). The guy was a murderer, a liar, and an adulterer. He betrayed a faithful friend in the most devious of ways. And yet God includes David in the very lineage of Jesus. That's a deep relationship.

David wrote many of the psalms, pouring his heart out to the Lord. They're not always pretty, though. He complains: "*I am weary with my crying; my throat is dry*" (Psalm 69:3). He asks God hard questions: "*Why do You stand afar off, O Lord? Why do You hide in times of trouble?*" (Psalm 10:1). And he gets frustrated: "*Why are you cast down, O my soul? And why are you disquieted within me?*" (Psalm 42:5). But his heart knows what intimacy with his Maker feels like. So when he's had a chance to vent honestly to the Lord, David always finds his way back to worship. He reminds his soul over and over again about who God is, what He has done for him in the past, and how worthy God is of his trust. This is the intimate connection that God is inviting each and every one of us into. He's not scared of our feelings or offended by our frustration. We can tell Him what we really think and feel, and then we can trust Him to meet us exactly where we are with His mercy and truth.

The entire Bible can be seen as one long love letter of God calling His people back into His loving embrace. The Lord doesn't just permit us to have an intimate relationship with Him; He pursues one with us. After my body was supernaturally healed, I was hungry to know this God who is real and has positive answers for today. I began to devour any sort of teaching on God's goodness, His promises, and how I could be closer to Him. This was around the time of the Toronto Blessing and the Brownsville Revival where I saw numerous people being touched by God's love and His power in radical ways. I cared about addressing my complicated sexuality, absolutely. But there was something much larger going on—I was being introduced to the God who invades the impossible, the God who heals diseases and who knows each of His kids intimately, who comes close to His children. I realized that He wanted to be with me, and that changed everything.

The relationship that He was drawing me into was one filled with compassion and tender love. Like the father in the story of the prodigal son, God is ready and waiting for us to run into His arms again. When we don't deserve it, He throws a robe over our shoulders and adorns us with identity and tender affection. The father in that parable didn't grill the son about his poor life choices; he grabbed him into his arms and threw him a welcome-home party. Our heavenly Father will buy an entire field of dirt for a single piece of treasure (see Matthew 13:44). He will leave the 99 sheep to go after the one who is lost (see Luke 15:4-7). His goodness and mercy are chasing after each one of us. *He* is chasing after us.

Intimacy Informs Identity

Jesus modeled for us the life that is possible when a man or woman is walking in the Spirit. John 14:12 says, *"whoever believes in me will do the works I have been doing, and they will do even greater things than these, because I am going to the Father"* (NIV). And throughout His time of ministry, we see Jesus prioritizing His intimate connection with the Father. He took time away from the crowds to pray (see Luke 5:16). He fasted (see Matthew 4:2). And, from this place of connection with His Father, He was able to see every darkness bow to the Kingdom of Heaven. Jesus knew who He was because He knew *whose* He was, and His life revealed the primacy of His relationship with God. It is the same for us.

My partner in ministry, Elizabeth Woning, said it well: "When you're really in the presence of the Lord, you can't help but to be yourself." The more time we spend in the presence of our Creator, the One who has numbered the very hairs on our heads, the more familiar we become with who He is. But we also start to see more clearly who He created us to be. And our sexual identity is a part of that. We cannot separate part of ourselves from our biology. He made us male or female, and it is through intimacy with Him that we begin to discover the fullness of who we are.

When I was striving for the attention of those other boys, I was desperately trying to define my identity by someone else. It wasn't until I began to see Scripture as an on-ramp to connect with the person of God that I could begin to feel His delight in me. The Bible became a crucial instruction tool that God had provided me. It was an offering of practical help from my loving Father. And the time I spent learning who the Bible said God was and what a life in Him looked like didn't

57

just give me helpful information; it made me feel safe—known. There were moments when it felt as though God's words to me in Scripture cost me something. Sometimes I needed to lay down an unhealthy behavior or belief. But those demands paled in comparison to the continuous feelings of His attentiveness and preference for me, which melted my self-hate. Where were my accusers? If God accepted me and was committed to discipling me, I must be valuable. I began to be able to see who I was through His eyes, and I could relearn how to meet the very legitimate emotional needs of my heart in the way He knew would give me the most life.

Jesus loves friendship. God designed us to not only need intimacy with Him, but to also need non-sexual, deep connection with other people. Looking at the life of Jesus, we can see how close He was with His friends and disciples. He lived with them and ate with them, He wept with Mary and Martha when their brother died, He went to parties, and He invited John—the one who said Jesus loved him most—to lay his head on His chest. His life was filled with life-giving, non-sexual intimacy. The source of His identity was the Father and, from that place of security, His love overflowed to those around Him.

Trusting Him

Liz Flaherty is a dear friend and a champion for sexual wholeness. Her story, shared below, is a powerful example of walking headlong into God's waiting arms. Because of the transformation she has experienced in her ability to receive God's love, she walks in incredible freedom today.

Deep in the mountains of Northern California rests the little town I grew up in. I'll call it Wilsonville. To this day, the small wooded community only houses about twelve hundred people. My parents left their high-paying jobs in Silicon Valley and relocated there to pastor a church of about five members when I was seven years old.

We big-city Christians contrasted sharply with the culture in this new place. As much as I am thankful for growing up in such a diverse and contrasting culture—rich with the arts, strong community unity despite their differences, and the benefits of growing up in the mountains—I unfortunately experienced much pain there. This was due to so many factors, one being that I experienced bullying and rejection trying to navigate those years. I was a very overweight and shy child, and being one of the few Christians in a postmodern culture only leant to feeling as more of an outsider. Coupled with my parents' never-ending financial hardship and their own personal struggles from growing up in abusive homes, I discovered that there was much pain to overcome in the world. In order to escape the pain, I eventually began to distrust God with my life and pursued other means of making sense of the world around me.

This included distancing myself from my faith, but also pursuing sexual relationships and drugs. Most of my attempts to form romantic relationships ended in heartache. I did have a few boyfriends, but nothing long term. And as you can imagine, these sexual experiences never led to anything resembling a fruitful relationship or even so much as a healthy friendship with a boy. I was trading myself for any sort of attention or validation I could get my hands on.

This process eventually wore me down, and going into my senior year of high school I became callous toward guys. More and more I realized that I was always more comfortable with, affirmed by, and safe around my girlfriends. The depth of intimacy and safety I felt with my close female friends was far greater than anything I had shared with a man. And when I was honest with myself, I found that I had experienced sexual attraction to girls since early on in puberty.

When the subject of homosexuality was spoken about in the church it was surrounded by disdain. So I locked it away and tried to navigate things on my own. However, one night when I was drunk with some friends, I had what I believed was my grand epiphany: I was a lesbian. It seemed like the pieces of the puzzle were finally coming together for me. I "came out" my senior year and shortly after that I left for college. I was finally free from all the drama and rejection of high school, and reveling in my newfound identity. For a while my life appeared to be perfect....

As I sat in my living room one afternoon, having smoked enough weed to choke a horse, I was suddenly overwhelmed by a realization of just how deep into this pit of depression I had fallen—how disconnected I was from my family and from God. So, I began to speak to Him. I told Him I wasn't sure if I was allowed to talk to Him while I was high, but I couldn't get myself out of this pit. Suddenly the room filled with the presence of God and all at once I knew that He truly loved me, even in my drug-induced state.

Unfortunately, my problems did not miraculously dissipate that afternoon, but I did experience a grace to stop smoking and drinking. Sober and newly committed to handing my life over to God, I reconciled with my family. I also felt led by God to enroll in a ministry school in another city. This new relationship with Him was all I cared about. I spent as much time as I could in prayer, worship, and Bible study. I learned a lot during this time and had experiences with God that I never thought were possible. And even during all this, I continued to experience same-sex attraction.

Seriously, Liz? Isn't this your mountaintop testimony? You submitted your life to God and still you were attracted to other women? Yup. Aligning myself with God's will allowed me to have powerful encounters with Him where a ton of torment left my soul, but the feelings and temptations were still there.

These unresolved feelings started to eat away at my thought life, and I began once more to blow my world up with poor choices after finishing ministry school. Thankfully, though, I was introduced to Living Waters, a sexual wholeness ministry, and the pieces of the puzzle started to come together in my soul. This ministry taught me what intimacy with Jesus really looked like, especially in regard to my sexuality. We were led by a married couple who had walked through many struggles in these areas. Once a week, we came together to form a loving environment where we could not only open up and receive counsel, but take in sound biblical teaching.

The class didn't place any huge expectations on us concerning our growth in our femininity or masculinity; the only requirement was that we stay connected to the Holy Spirit and follow Christ.

We were primarily taught how to have an intimate relationship with Jesus by completely depending on the work of Jesus in our daily lives. We were loved by people who were imperfect, who let us be our messy selves, and who encouraged us to grow without measuring our progress against some man-made standard. Our leaders understood the foundational teachings of the Gospel: repentance, forgiveness, and receiving His grace to walk out obedience. The Gospel allows for intimacy because we learn to trust the one who loves us. In this place of trust, intimacy blooms and results in the fruit of the Spirit.

"But the fruit of the Spirit is love, joy, peace, longsuffering, kindness, goodness, faithfulness, gentleness, self-control" (Galatians 5:22). As Paul goes on to say in verse 25, *"If we live in the Spirit, let us also walk in the Spirit."* The phrase *"walk in the spirit"* actually means to walk in line with, which is to walk along the path the Lord lays down for us. You can't follow someone you don't trust.

In this process of learning how to follow and trust Jesus, it produced an intimacy that allowed for peace to flow in my life. From this place of intimacy, I began to see all the places I needed to repent of in my way of thinking and living. Repenting meant allowing the Holy Spirit to identify thought patterns that did not align with His truth and receiving what He had to say about these areas of my life.

This sounds pretty simple, but it's anything but easy; this process is costly because transformation is invasive and extensive. It takes truly letting go and trusting Him. It takes meditating on the Word and spending many hours dialoguing with Him, when sometimes all you want to do is pick up the reins of your life and take control again. It takes your entire self. It's painful and beautiful. Intimacy with Jesus is a moment by moment decision that only you can make, and your life will be filled with the fruit of His likeness if you trust Him.

I'm overcome with thankfulness for all the Lord has restored in my life. I have a fruitful marriage of over fifteen years, I'm able to engage in healthy friendships with women without falling into old traps of codependency, and I'm free from the addiction of pornography. In my wildest dreams, I never knew I could be this free. Jesus is truly remarkable and worthy of pouring out our lives to Him. He is faithful.[1]

Scripture puts it like this:

We can all draw close to him with the veil removed from our faces. And with no veil we all become like mirrors who brightly reflect the glory of the Lord Jesus. We are being transfigured into his very image as we move from one brighter level of glory to another. And this glorious transfiguration comes from the Lord, who is the Spirit (2 Corinthians 3:18 TPT).

When we lift the veil, allowing God's access into the most intimate areas of our hearts, we become more like Him. The Bible doesn't say that we transform ourselves; we're not that powerful. He does that. It is His Spirit—not our own effort—that transforms us. Our job is to follow His leadings and receive the transformative power of His love and grace. He does the rest.

My brilliant pastor, Bill Johnson, says, "God loves you just the way you are. But He loves you too much to leave you that way." Our journey with God is just that—a journey. He is continuously leading us to be closer to Him, thereby transforming us to align with His Word. He loves us unconditionally but also loves us too much to not help us change and grow. When we eagerly pursue our own relationship with the Lord, we allow Him to mold and change us. Each person's path is unique. Along the way, we all experience moments of temptation that try to steal our hope and whisper lies to us about our identities. But if we keep our eyes on Him, instead of our own sin, *"He who has begun a good work in you will complete it"* (Philippians 1:6). The only way to fail is to quit.

Note

1. Liz Flaherty, "Intimacy Requires Trust," in *Finding You*: *An Identity-Based Journey Out of Homosexuality and Into All Things New* (2020).

Chapter 3

CHANGE IS POSSIBLE

At some level, those of us who have struggled with same-sex attraction have experienced a disruption in intimacy. And today, those who have made this reality known to the public by openly identifying as LGBTQ risk aligning themselves with an entire subculture that celebrates beliefs and behaviors that are contrary to biblical morality. Being daily influenced by others within that impassioned world may have created strong bonds, beliefs, and experiences that require attention from the Lord. So, as I spoke about in the previous chapter, transformation and resolution can be a journey. But it doesn't matter what has happened to us or what we have done; we do not have to walk this out alone. God longs to lead us on this intimacy journey. We don't have to figure out exactly what to do. We don't even have to know how to "properly" pursue intimacy with God. The Bible promises that the Holy Spirit will lead us into all truth (see John 16:13). So we can merely relax and accept that there are many potential aspects of our lives that could be factors in our same-sex attraction; we don't need to have it all figured out in order to take steps forward.

This next statement might be the most painful one I will make in this book for those with the homosexual experience. It is this: change is possible. I remember the agony of wrestling with homosexuality—with same-sex arousals—and the shame and confusion it brought. I lived with rejection and self-hatred every day. Many of us who have experienced this pain find it terrifying to hope for change of our understanding of who we are and who we desire. But the reality is that I couldn't have arrived at the peace and fulfillment I now enjoy without hearing this truth from a few people in my life who were able to testify that genuine, lasting transformation is available.

With the world screaming the opposite, I feel even more compelled to say that there *are* people who are experiencing dramatic change. We won't seek out breakthrough for our own lives if we don't know it's possible. There is no condemnation for anyone, regardless of the attraction he/she is experiencing. No one needs to change one bit to experience my respect and love. That anyone would endeavor to follow God closely each day is admirable. But I cannot diminish the truth. I am compelled to proclaim that my friends and I have experienced change. Change is possible.

The very core of the Gospel carries the message of transformation. Christ came to earth to remove us from the predictable bondage of sin, illness, and death. He came to set us free so that, in our freedom, we could unite with Him and be transformed into our true identities—sons and daughters who resemble their Father. When Jesus went to the cross, He made no exceptions. He didn't die for most sins or offer redemption to everyone except for a select few. His sacrifice rocked the world to such an extent that the sun disappeared, the rocks split, and dead people roamed above ground (see Matthew 27). The cross changed everything. All of us are invited to receive the overwhelming grace of His Gospel. So, it shouldn't come as a surprise that, because of that grace, our weaknesses do not escape His notice—not even our weaknesses in our identities and sexuality. Jesus came for *all* to be set free, for *all* to know Him, for *all* to experience the peace and transformative power of His Kingdom.

And He's not offended by our journey of transformation. When we hand over our lives to the Lord, repenting and receiving His love, we are immediately included in the Body of Christ. The salvation of our souls is immediate. But our sanctification—the process by which we grow to look like Jesus—takes time. Some people may experience immediate transformation in certain areas of their lives when they are born again. Maybe they suddenly don't feel so quick to anger, they might be set free from an addiction, or their self-centered motivations shift. This change is a beautiful thing. But all of us will have areas of our lives that require time to transform.

Look at the disciples. For three years, they spent every moment with Jesus, sharing the message of the Gospel and seeing miracle after miracle happen in front of their eyes. And yet Peter clearly had some issues with impulse control, James and John let their resentment rule so much that they tried to destroy a whole city with fire, and all of the disciples competed over who was the best.

Jesus knew their weaknesses before He ever chose them. He saw each disciple for who he was—warts and all—and He loved each completely. Each time they made a boneheaded move, Jesus corrected them, guiding them back to His perspective. He didn't reject them or give up on them; He merely invested time in retraining their thinking to His perspective. That retraining is what He is offering each one of us. Jesus is not afraid of our messy process. All true followers of Christ are traveling a lifelong journey of increasing our spiritual maturity. God is not impatient with us. He simply provides us with the tools we need and guides us with His Holy Spirit to the extent that we are ready and willing to allow His intervention into our lives.

Change Is Necessary

It's not for His sake alone that God invests so much in our transformation. Sin isn't some annoying behavior that irks the Lord, so He'd prefer it if we'd stop. Sin destroys us, isolates us, and lies to us about who we are. It is for *our* benefit that Jesus longs for those of us who are engaging in homosexual sex to step out of behaviors that bring us harm and into the freedom found in His way of life. He knows us better than we know ourselves. Some may think that Christianity offers an arbitrary, antiquated biblical demand handed down from a bunch of old men who hadn't yet experienced sexual freedom. But the opposite is true. Modern science is continuously discovering and proving the truth of the Bible.

Today, Hollywood loves to portray the gay lifestyle as one big party, but the reality is that most people involved in this way of life are navigating incredible pain. Biologically, homosexual activity has proven to wreak havoc on the minds and bodies of participants. Men who have sex with men have increased risks compared to men who do not have sex with men. They have an average life expectancy reduced by 20 years, make up more than half of the population of those diagnosed with HIV, and are much more likely to experience emotional turmoil—cases of mood and anxiety disorders, substance abuse, depression, and suicide attempts.[1,2,3] Similarly, gender dysphoria—the condition of experiencing one's psychological identity to be different from one's biological sex—is leading men and women to irreparably damage their bodies through cross-sex hormones and cosmetic surgeries. Sexual identity is written into our beings at a chromosomal level and cannot be altered. Without addressing the root causes of the pain and confusion about their sexuality, these precious individuals are being sold a fake cure. And, when their pain is not alleviated, they are still 19 times more likely to commit suicide than the average person. Statistically, their condition has not improved despite embracing transgender identity at extreme lengths.[4]

Psychologically, many of us who have struggled with same-sex attraction also experience self-hatred, emotional pain, codependency, isolation, and an insecurity among same-sex peers. We didn't seek same-sex desires out. Yet, relationships and family members begin to pay a price, in various ways, for our decision to live in contrast to who we were created to be. Cases of domestic violence are higher in same-sex relationships.[5] I know that there are many gay-identified people who have adopted children into their families and are providing them with lots of love. But men and women are different in so many ways, and these children do miss out on the blessing of being covered and nurtured by both a mother and a father. Over 2,500 studies indicate a married man and woman raising their own children offer clear advantages to those kids that no other family structure can.[6]

For years, the argument in support of the gay lifestyle was that some people were just born that way, and there was nothing that could be done about it. Scientifically, however, we continue to learn that this just isn't the case. The recent Ganna Study (a 30-year collaboration among scientists at Harvard, MIT, and other reputable universities) has shed some conclusive evidence on this argument. After studying the entire human genome of 493,001 individuals over a 30-year period, they have conclusively stated that, while there are some genetic correlations (as would be expected with such a study), they found no isolated gene or genes that caused homosexuality. The study indicated that homosexual behavior cannot be predicted by looking exclusively at an individual's genes, nobody develops a homosexual identity or behavior without the overwhelming influence of environmental factors, and gay-identified people have a completely normal human genome.[7]

These may be new discoveries for us, but they are not surprising to God. He knows the pain and negative impacts upon us and those around us when we act against our original design. That is why, in the Bible, homosexuality is always a condemned behavior. There isn't one example of a homosexual relationship being blessed by God. He reserves that blessing for marriage between a man and a woman. The Lord is not condemning those of us who have struggled with same-sex attraction; He is offering us a way out. These advances in science are not only discovering the truth about the effects of homosexual behavior, they are also uncovering the hope that God hard-wired into our very beings. Advances in brain science have revealed that the pathways in our brains—our reactions to certain stimuli, our emotional responses, our choices—can absolutely change. This is called neuroplasticity. There is no stagnant "us." God calls each one of us to lay down our lives and be born again. Jesus did not come to condemn the world, but to save it (see John 3:17). And He will meet us exactly where we are. He will take us by the hand and lead us out, into His freedom.

Change Is Life Giving

Experiencing sexual abuse as a young child, my spiritual son Gabriel Pagan grew up believing that acting out sexually was the way that he was going to get love from father figures. He grew up in a religious household, believing that he was gay, that God hated gay people, and that he was going to hell. But Gabriel met Jesus and realized that He still wanted connection with him even in his immaturity and sinfulness. His connection with God changed everything.

I used to be very depressed and constantly paranoid of what people thought about me. I explored sexuality in high school after being exposed to sexual activity and pornography as a kid. Acting out through masturbation and webcams became an obsessive habit to which I lost all control. It got to the point where I was acting out what I was seeing on screens in public.

This brought me to my lowest point, and I wanted to kill myself. I was unaware that people were praying for me, but because they did, I felt motivated to change my life. Someone reached out to me on social media and shared Jesus with me. I accepted Jesus Christ in my driveway, and the Holy Spirit fell on me like fire which brought me through a series of encounters. I went through a Bethel Sozo (listening prayer-type) ministry and saw Jesus holding me that first time I was touched inappropriately, and I told the Lord that I would never sleep with another man if I had His presence like that forever.

Gabriel knew that he was in pain, but he didn't escape that pain by simply trying to manage the sexual expression of that pain. Instead of embracing the shame about his behavior, he began to focus on the presence and love of God. He realized that he could have a personal relationship with the Creator, with the very source of true intimacy and identity.

When Gabriel began to get to know this personal God, he began to experience real, radical love. And he began to see that God was inviting him to experience a full life with Him. He began to do outreach with his church and even went on a mission trip to Haiti.

"Everything in my life flipped upside down. I went from being a depressed, addicted, partier metal-head...[to being] on a mission trip, praying for friends, casting out demons, and seeing the Bible come alive." His understanding of God was shifting dramatically, and he began to learn how to recognize His voice. He realized that God didn't want him to live a small, boring, restricted life. God was inviting him to live like Jesus. He dove into learning how to hear God's voice, and he connected with a pastoral counselor to walk through his pain and addiction.

Fully embarked on his intimate journey with God, one day Gabriel was on an outreach with his church in his city. He was praying for a homeless man and, afterward, wrapped his arms around the man, telling him how much Jesus loved him. Suddenly, he found himself aroused. Confused and freaked out, he wondered what had just happened. He'd been experiencing breakthroughs in his sexual identity, and this interaction hadn't felt sexual up until that moment.

> I heard a voice say, "See, God didn't save you. You're still a f—ing f—got." But my pastor raised me on understanding that the voice of God is your biggest security besides the Word of God.
>
> So, I said, "Holy Spirit, because this happened to my body, does this mean I'm gay?"
>
> And I heard, "Son, do not listen to that voice. It came from a demon. I did deliver you." And, so, Jesus taught me how to trust Him [even] when my body said everything else.

Gabriel landed on a valuable tool for this journey—his focus. If he had made his physical reactions the focus of his journey, that moment on outreach would have sidetracked him. But God was able to tell him otherwise. When we are desiring to separate ourselves entirely from the homosexual experience, there are so many layers of restoration happening within us. We cannot glare at our behavior or desires and expect them to change automatically. Our main motivator must be intimacy with God.

No matter where we are along our path—at the very beginning of considering change or having experienced incredible breakthrough in the areas of identity and intimacy—there is grace for everyone. And there is certainly grace for those of us who have been pursuing the Lord but have yet to experience any transformation in this area of our lives. But if you are pursuing God for wholeness and freedom, I want you to know that there is hope. Gabriel's testimony and the testimony of thousands of others who have been transformed by God's love prophesy to this fact: Hope is alive, and God has more than enough grace for each of our journeys. Today, Gabriel is happily married to a woman and they just had their first child.[8]

> Seven years later and I'm free from being bound to same-sex attractions. I'm happy and living a wild life of adventure following Jesus Christ. Today I live knowing that what once brought me the most shame is completely taken away by a God who didn't avoid my pain or questions. I serve as a pastor at my local church and lead people through inner healing sessions. My greatest joy is seeing Jesus crush unbelief by stepping into people's pain and watching them encounter the God who kept me from ending my own life. I was addicted and now I'm free. I was depressed and now I'm full of joy. I was full of hate and now I'm moved by love.[9]

Change Is Happening

In early 2018, Elizabeth Woning and I, as a part of our ministry, began to get involved in opposing an assembly bill in the state of California referred to as AB2943. This bill proposed to outlaw the very books, resources, and counseling that had saved my life. Any conference, counseling modality, or literature that suggested that leaving behind a homosexual orientation was possible was on the chopping block. They argued that sexual orientation change was fraudulent. So the promotion of that kind of material would become fraudulent itself under California's consumer protection laws. Counseling choice was already illegal in California for minors, but now an adult wouldn't be able to receive ministry, therapy, or resources even if they were personally requesting it.

Legislation was being passed worldwide, not merely securing rights for LGBTQ-identified people, but taking away the rights of adults who were not content to live out homosexual desires. In some cases, our testimonies had been sanctioned, our social media accounts had been censored or shut down, and newspapers and TV news spewed personal attacks. Many of us had come to experience same-sex attraction or confusion about our sexual identity as a direct result of emotional, physical, or sexual abuse. So I knew that protecting our rights to receive counseling and other help in a way that lined up with our faith convictions was paramount. Realizing how crucial those kinds of resources had been to our own journeys of transformation, Elizabeth and I jumped into action to share our personal stories.

Looking to lend our support to those contesting this bill, we soon found ourselves taking the witness stand and sharing our testimonies in legislative committee hearings. Having gone through five years of weekly professional Christian counseling and various ministries, I was able to share how this bill would have removed my freedom to pursue emotional healing and happiness. After hearing several testimonies from people who had left a homosexual life behind, the state Assembly majority leader stood up and said, "You know, I just don't believe any of this." Unconvinced by our testimonies, the Assembly members kept the bill moving forward.

Discouraged, on a drive home from a hearing, I turned to Elizabeth and said, "We need a book of testimonies. These legislators have never personally met anyone who's changed!" With the full support of our church's leadership, we began to plan a book that could be printed before the bill would pass by a senate vote only weeks later. To do that, though, we'd have to collect dozens of written testimonies within the following five days.

As the book creation process was beginning, we were invited to the first-ever Freedom March happening in Washington, D.C. Organized by Jeffrey McCall, the Freedom March was a chance for people who formerly identified as LGBTQ to publicly worship the Lord and share the good news of the transformation that Jesus had manifested in their lives. The organizers had heard Elizabeth and me testifying against AB2943, and they invited us to join them in Washington. We bought airline tickets immediately and flew out three days later. Suddenly, we were surrounded by people who had left homosexuality. In about six weeks, with the help of some amazing people, we held in our hands the first copies of *CHANGED: #oncegay Stories*. Anticipating the vote on the bill, we invited our new friends from the Freedom March to a rally in Sacramento.

There, we went door to door, handing signed copies of the book to each of the 40 state senators' offices, talking to them openly about how our people group—oncegay people—would be affected by AB2943.

Humbly, we tried to explain that adults should have the freedom to pursue the counseling that aligns with their beliefs. Erasing options for counseling and resources was discriminatory. Elizabeth again testified as part of a senate hearing along with our oncegay friend Jim Domen of Church United, and over 400 people supporting us each stepped up to the public microphone toward the end of the hearing, stating their names and vocalizing "I oppose this bill." It was one of the largest public responses ever in a California senate hearing.

Even with all of that, the senate passed the bill. It would now pass through a couple of formalities before almost certainly being signed into law.

The assemblyman who sponsored the bill, a gay-identified man himself and the head of the California LGBT caucus, though, had listened to our stories, and he surprisingly decided to speak to several groups of pastors across California to hear their perspectives. As a result of those conversations and what must have been the influence of God Himself, shockingly, without warrant, and with zero legal requirement, when the bill was within a couple hours of being passed with a final vote, the assemblyman pulled the bill. AB2943 would not become law.

Surprised and relieved, we realized that God had used this bill like a magnet, drawing former-LGBTQ believers together, organizing us to share our stories, and uniting the Body of Christ. The momentum from that time has continued to open up conversations—inside and outside of the four walls of the church—about homosexuality, creating safe spaces for encouragement, growth, and civic engagement. Since creating our website (changedmovement.com), we have sold thousands of copies of the *CHANGED: #oncegay Stories* book and launched an Instagram account (@changedmvmt) so that we could share these testimonies freely with the world. Every week, we continue to receive more stories of individuals experiencing new peace and fulfillment they didn't experience inside their LGBTQ worlds. We also have a closed Facebook group that now has thousands of people gathered testifying of Jesus' love and intervention and encouraging one another. And it's only just begun. God is on the move, ushering in a movement of sexual purity and wholeness that will not be stopped.

Bob Jones, a respected prophet, foresaw this moment in time. In 1989, he had an encounter with God in which he saw 100,000 people being set free from homosexuality. He saw HIV being healed and those transformed individuals dedicating their lives entirely to the Lord. From that initial wave of people breaking free from homosexuality, there would be a ripple effect of revival. "They will be totally dedicated. I saw 100,000 coming into the Kingdom. There's no telling how many that 100,000 will impact.... They will be like new. It will be all about Jesus. Some will become doctors. They will serve the Body of Christ. We need these people."

Truly believing this prophetic word was from God, and feeling His encouragement, I realized that I needed to expedite my dream of sharing my journey of transformation in a way that other people could take as their own. For years, I had been praying that God would show me how to communicate clearly the ways He had moved in my life—how He was eager to love and meet persons wrestling with their sexuality. I knew He'd done a work but hadn't analyzed how He'd done it. One morning, in the shower, it hit me. Like, I literally jumped out of the shower to write down what the Lord was saying to me. There were six keys to my transformation.

1. Vulnerability
2. Surrender
3. Relationships

4. Identity

5. Enduring Faith

6. Vision

Clearly, I saw how God had led me into vulnerability—learning to be seen and known by God and others—and then how I'd had to truly decide to surrender my life to His lordship. He showed me how He'd built healthy relationships around me, how He had invited me into a new identity in Him, and how He'd instilled an enduring faith to help me navigate the highs and lows of my journey into wholeness. And finally, the Lord showed me how I could change my future by catching His vision for my life and choosing not to believe a different report.

These six keys may not be in the perfect order for everyone, and there may be some keys that resonate more than others. But it took all of them for me to experience the dramatic transformation that the Lord led me into.

There is no formula or one-size-fits-all plan for how God leads us into wholeness and freedom. He's omnipotent, He's omniscient, and He interacts with us individually and intimately. So these six keys are offered here as probable doors of breakthrough, areas of invitation for God's transformative grace. His love can reach into any place in our hearts to bring His affection, truth, and peace. It's what He's done for me and countless others.

Notes

1. "CDC Fact Sheet: HIV Among Gay and Bisexual Men," Center for Disease Control, July 24, 2020, https://www.cdc.gov/nchhstp/newsroom/docs/factsheets/cdc-msm-508.pdf.

2. Mark Messih, M.D., M.SC., "Mental Health Facts for Gay Populations," American Psychiatric Association, 2018.

3. Robert S. Hogg, et al., "Modelling the Impact of HIV Disease on Mortality in Gay and Bisexual Men," *International Journal of Epidemiology*, International Epidemiological Association, (volume 26, no. [3]) October, 1996.

4. Neil Whitehead, "Homosexuality & Comorbidities," *Journal of Human Sexuality* 2:124-175, 2010.

5. Susan Jones, "Domestic Violence in LGBT Relationships Targeted," October 20, 2004, CNSNews.com.

6. Paul Strand, "Cause and Effect: The Benefits of Traditional Marriage," *CBN News,* The Christian Broadcasting Network, April 5, 2006.

7. Andrea Ganna, et al., "Large-Scale GWAS Reveals Insights into the Genetic Architecture of Same-Sex Behavior," *Science,* American Association for the Advancement of Science, (volume number 365, no. [6456]) August 30, 2019, https://science.sciencemag.org/content/365/6456/eaat7693.

8. Testimony: Gabriel Pagan, "Sex. Church. Culture. Vol 2: Stories and Solutions," online conference, 2020, https://www.moralrevolution.com/sex-church-culture-vol-ii.

9. Gabriel Pagan, *CHANGED: #oncegay Stories,* https://changedmovement.com/stories/gabriel-pagan.

Chapter 4

VULNERABILITY

We are hardwired for connection. God designed us to need not only Him, but also one another. Adam walked in the Garden with God, talking to Him like a friend, co-creating with Him. It sounds like Heaven. What more could he have possibly needed? But it was God who said that it wasn't good for Adam to be alone (see Genesis 2:18). It was God who made a partner for man—a woman who would know him intimately. Because that's the thing about connection. We can't experience intimacy fully until we allow ourselves to be seen and known.

For those of us who have been struggling with unwanted same-sex attraction, that idea is most likely terrifying. Often, we feel out of control, scared, and unknown. We don't want others to fully see us because we are hiding our pain, hidden sins, and maybe sexual interactions. For most of us, that is the stuff that gets kept quiet. But in my experience, it is often exactly where the journey should begin.

As a culture, we are becoming more and more comfortable with the word *vulnerability*, but the true meaning of the term often passes us by. We see people being "vulnerable" on social media by posting images of their dirty dishes sitting in the sink or admitting bad attitudes they'd had but overcome. That may be transparency—allowing people to see something that is happening in their lives—but vulnerability goes so much deeper. True vulnerability is the act of exposing your heart in such a way that it becomes possible for another person to wound you. No wonder it's terrifying.

Dr. Brené Brown is a personal hero in this arena. She has spent many years studying shame, vulnerability, and human connection. After years of statistical research, she has become a proponent for the vital importance of vulnerability. She explains that vulnerability requires the courage to be imperfect, the willingness to "tell the story of who you are with your whole heart."[1] Despite the cultural messages that we, and especially men, receive from the world, vulnerability is not weakness. It is emotional risk, she explains, but it is also "our most accurate measurement of courage...it is the birthplace of innovation, creativity, and change."[2] It is a prerequisite for true connection and a full life.

We were created by Love Himself to feel loved unconditionally. Not everyone experiences this, though. Many people who come to me asking for help with addressing their sexual identity issues approach me with a demeanor that says "all is well." They've been so accustomed to hiding their true feelings that they even put up a façade when meeting with me, the person who is supposed to help them. This façade slows my ability to help them to experience God's unconditional love, which is the most transformative, powerful force in the universe. They can't experience that love if they keep themselves walled off.

I like to remind people that you'll never know unconditional love until you've first shared your condition. It is through vulnerability that we can experience God's intention for restoration. The minute we go tell a trusted friend that we've, for example, slipped up again with pornography and then repent, our slate is wiped clean. We have the opportunity to begin that very moment identifying again as the saint—the brand-new creation—that Jesus' crucifixion and resurrection offers to us.

A spiritual father of mine, Prophet Kris Vallotton, has a brilliant teaching on authentic confession. He explains that vulnerable confession is the first step toward healing and restoration. "Authenticity leads to confession," he says, "which brings wholeness." The Bible tells us to confess our sins *"that you may be healed"* (James 5:16). It also says that, *"If we confess our sins, He is faithful and just to forgive us our sins and to cleanse us from all unrighteousness"* (1 John 1:9). Kris teaches that vulnerable confession doesn't fix everything on its own, but it begins this process of cleansing. When we admit our fault with authentic vulnerability, God will uproot whatever heart issue led us into sin in the first place. Some people get addicted to confessing—experiencing the relief that unburdening themselves brings without actually changing their behavior. But true confession needs to lead to genuine repentance. "Confession breaks the power of sin," Kris explains, "but repentance connects me to the power of grace." When we choose to be vulnerable with the people we trust and with the Lord, we get to receive complete forgiveness. Our sins have been washed away, and God brings healing.[3]

When I was in high school, we had this miniature Maltese dog named Missy. One day, we came back home to find Missy catatonic in the kitchen. The poor little thing wasn't her playful self. She was frozen stiff—one hundred percent intense, not blinking nearly enough, and possibly not breathing; we couldn't tell. We had no idea what was going on! Soon, though, the empty marshmallow bag gave her away.

Our little princess had "sinned." She'd eaten her weight in marshmallows. You could say that she had quite literally stuffed herself. And, like the rest of us with a conscience, soon she couldn't keep it all inside any longer. Before we could even figure out whether she was in any danger, her little body decided that it was time to "confess." Her swollen belly began to heave, at which point her mouth flew open, and Missy began to pump marshmallow cream out onto the floor. Wide-eyed, we watched this humiliating little "confession" for about a minute as liquid marshmallow continued to flow. But just as suddenly as it had begun, it stopped. Missy, now free from the pressure of what was making her sick, was instantly back to her happy, normal self.

It's a silly example, but this is what vulnerability can be like. If we do it the way God has instructed us, we can be free of the sin and shame. We can release the things that have been infecting us, allowing God's love to pour in and restore us to our original design. It can be scary and get messy, but the peace and freedom are so worth it.

Out of Hiding

The alternative to vulnerability is a life of hiding and disconnection. It's natural to want to hide our mistakes. Adam and Eve hid from God, feeling suddenly exposed by their own bad choices (see Genesis 3:8). But once we start hiding our hearts out of fear, we also stop receiving the love and connection that we need. Let's say I'm at church, praying for people on the prayer line, and someone comes up to me to encourage me. They say, "You're such a great man of God. God loves you so much, Ken. I'm so impressed with you."

If I've been living a life of unconfessed sin, not being vulnerable regarding my failures, then all those life-giving words fall to the floor. I automatically shut my heart down from receiving those words of affirmation. Because of my own shame and hiddenness, I will push away the very words of love that God intended to encourage and heal me. I think to myself, "If this guy knew who I am or what I did last week, he wouldn't value me or be saying these nice things about me." My lack of vulnerability would create a barrier between my heart and God's unconditional love, isolating me in my sin and further subjecting me to the influence of the accuser of the brethren, satan.

When we choose to live courageously—stepping into vulnerability—freedom and healing are our rewards. Sometimes we are in such pain that we can explode onto whoever happens to be nearby. But moving into vulnerability with wisdom looks like intentionally choosing the person/people with whom we share our pain. We want to choose people who are trustworthy, who will cover us and be able to handle the information we share with them. But we also want to be vulnerable with people who share our Christian core values regarding righteousness. It can be tempting, if we're new to vulnerability, to share our sin only with people who will brush it off and appease our conscience. Instead, we need to choose people who will speak the truth in love—those who also know that God's best plan for us is not to pursue homosexuality.

We want to make sure we are choosing to be vulnerable with people who, themselves, are godly people and will lead us in the right direction. Elizabeth Woning says it this way:

> Allowing ourselves to be seen in this way with trustworthy friends breaks the power of shame that makes us feel rejected by others, and also gives us a standard (our true identity) to live up to. While shame can make us feel there is something hidden (unknown even to ourselves) that causes others to reject us, vulnerability allows us to belong, being fully seen. It creates the opportunity to walk together with others authentically. Finally, we can be

ourselves! And begin to really see ourselves as the man or woman God created us to be.

Carmen Vaught, a good friend of mine, experienced the power of vulnerability in her journey out of lesbianism:

> Life for me felt out of control. It was a constant battle to find peace in who I was and to prove I was good. When I started to have feelings for other girls, confusion entered in. I had no safe place to talk about it, and I believed the shame I carried would only grow if I admitted how I was feeling. Because I was not like other girls and felt rejected by guys I liked, I felt unworthy in my femininity. In my early 20s I began meeting people in the LGBTQ community, and I felt like I finally fit in.
>
> This community championed me to come out. As I ran into the arms of this so-called love, my shame and self-hatred actually grew, and I felt that people in the Church and my family also hated me. I thought that, if my family would just accept my sexuality, then I would be at peace and life would be amazing.
>
> After twelve years of family heartache and separation, they started to express their love and admiration for me and to express their desire for relationship. I knew they didn't agree with my lifestyle, yet I felt their love for me. I thought I'd be ecstatic about that, but I actually found myself thinking, "Maybe I don't accept this life for myself."
>
> Six months later, my girlfriend of three years was cheating on me and moved out. I was miserable. The life I had pursued to find fulfillment left me at rock bottom instead. I was so

scared to walk away from that identity because I didn't know who I was without it. I finally told God, "I have no idea who I am, but You created me so You're going to have to tell me."

I decided to go back to church. On my first visit, I noticed an announcement for "a Christ-centered healing and support group for those seeking truth and grace in their sexuality and relationship with God." I attended the first meeting and when it was my turn to share why I was there, all I could say through my tears was "self-worth." This ministry was my place of healing. For the first time in my life, I felt like I could share my pain with others. We met for several months, uncovering the wounded places, and they loved me every step of the way, even in my mess. This kind of love offered me hope, not just something to numb my pain.

As I looked to Jesus, my heart changed, and I began to understand who God created me to be. I accepted a relationship with Him, not a set of rules. Now the internal battle is over, and I can walk in peace in my true identity. I love who I am and that I'm different from a lot of women. My life now has so much purpose. I get to use my profession of photography in ministry, travel around the world, and bring hope to others with my story of God's love. His plans are way better than anything I ever imagined![4]

Breaking Shame

The major barrier to the healing power of vulnerability is shame. Shame lies to us, telling us that we're not worthy of love because of what we've done. It focuses on tearing down our identity until we are repeating the lie, "I am bad," instead of feeling the genuine conviction that says, "I did something bad." But here's the truth: Jesus Christ came to set us free from all shame and condemnation (see Romans 8:1). Once we give our lives to Jesus, we have a champion of righteousness on our side. The Holy Spirit comforts us, guiding us into the truth that will set us free. He turns us back from the sinful behavior that would destroy us, offering redemption at every turn.

These were new thoughts for me when I was navigating my struggle with my sexual identity during my ministry school years. At least, I'd never really believed these truths before. I began to meet with a man also named "Ken." For a few years, he met with me regularly to help me. He had lived a gay lifestyle but had gone on his own journey to wholeness and was leading a Living Waters program (the same ministry my friend Liz mentioned in Chapter 2) for people battling sexual and relational problems, which I attended. On one particular Saturday, he brought up the concept of shame, and he began to teach me about my identity as a son of God. The things he was saying were remarkable, and they lifted a weight off of me. I went home thinking about this new revelation and wrote the following in my journal:

> I had a nice day today. I met with Ken...at 4:00 for over an hour. He seems to be 100% free from all homosexual tendency and says that he is. He assures me I can be, as well. He felt like the main thing I needed to get free of today was shame. He reminded me of how, after Romans 7, Paul says (in Romans 8:1) that there is no condemnation to those in Christ Jesus. He said that I needed to rest, rest, rest. I needed to recognize that I am OK with God, just as I am. I already have as much favor as I am ever gonna get

from Him. I can't get any more. I need to imagine myself being OK with Him, and having Him hold me. The emotional point for me was when he told me that God didn't expect me to know how to be perfect. That was the job of a father—to show me the way. So, it was real freeing and broke the shame off of me to know that God didn't expect me to be perfect. Also, he asked me if I understood that it was sin for me to view myself other than the way God views me. He said that God didn't like it when people harm His kids or mess with their souls. So, I need to repent and refrain from viewing myself as anything other than being redeemed by the blood of Jesus.

God didn't just care about my behavior, He cared about my heart. He wanted me to bring Him all of my failures, all of my sexual sins, all of the false identities I had adopted. His desire was for me to lay it all at His feet so that He could remove the burden of sin from my life and restore me to His freedom. My job wasn't to be the perfect Christian; my job was to open up my heart to the transformative power of God's grace. I was no longer guilty. Jesus had taken that to the cross. I could release my shame into Jesus' trustworthy hands and let His strength invade every area of weakness in my life.

Repentance and Confession

The Holy Spirit never shames us for our areas of pain or sin, but He does empower us as we become more and more like Jesus. And this doesn't happen without the vulnerable actions of confessing the pain and sin in our lives and turning to receive God's mercy. The Bible tells us to confess both to one another and to the Lord. Scripture is filled with verses encouraging us to confess our sins, but there is always a promise attached to that action. If we confess our sins, God will forgive us. He will show us mercy (see Proverbs 28:13). He will lift up those who humble themselves (see James 4:10).

Confession and repentance begin with experiencing regret for something we've done. This is not the same as shame. It's healthy to grieve and allow ourselves to feel disappointed in our behavior, but it doesn't end there. Repentance means "to turn," so when we feel the conviction of the Holy Spirit, we can take our sorrow to the Lord and to anyone else whom we've hurt, allowing the vulnerable posture of confession to work its way in us. We confess, we ask for forgiveness from the Lord and others, and then we turn from that behavior and head back in the direction of freedom.

For those of us who are currently working toward wholeness in the realm of sexuality, there are a few common areas of repentance that are often needed. The first is pride. Often, when we've been hiding in shame so deeply, we can build a protective edifice of pride over our hearts as a way to cover the shame. It's too painful to consider how sinful we have been, so we unknowingly manufacture our own affirmation, considering ourselves better than others. Pride often manifests in our lives as offense and anger. Without turning from pride, we won't be able to submit to the lordship of Jesus and allow His love to touch us. Confessing and repenting from lust or sexual sin is also an important focus. If we don't distance ourselves from sexual sin in this way, the enemy can use that against us, bringing shame and condemnation, halting our growth and ability to receive all of God's healing love.

It's not only sin, though, that is released through confession. As we step out on this journey to wholeness, there are deep pockets of emotional pain in our hearts that can be released. The Lord will often allow that pain to bubble up to the surface as we step into vulnerability so that it can receive the tender compassion from others that brings resolution. When we find people whom we can trust, we can open up these areas of pain to them, allowing the Lord to speak His truth and love into the situation.

It was very painful for me when the kids at school called me names, but years later when I shared that with people I trusted, I was able to hear them say, "I'm so sorry, Ken, that those kids called you a faggot on the playground when you were in elementary school. That's not who you are. I don't see you that way; you are a valiant man of God." And in this simple, compassionate exchange, I was able to release that festering area of pain and nail it to the cross. All of the injustice and cruelty we have ever experienced was carried to the cross by Jesus Christ. And as we release our hold on our own pain and hand it over to Him, we can participate in the redemptive work of His resurrection.

The Payoff

On the other side of the discomfort of vulnerability, a life of increased intimacy with both God and people lies waiting. That's what my friend Andrew Franklin has discovered, and it has changed the course of his life. Andrew grew up struggling in secret with same-sex attraction. He was raised in the church and heard people gossip about the sexuality of other church members. Fearing rejection, he buried his feelings and turned to fantasy and masturbation. But it wasn't a happy life. "I didn't have any joy, because I was under the weight of all of my secrets." He cried out to God to fix him, but nothing changed.

Once he went to college, he saw people living an openly homo-sexual lifestyle. Attracted to a life without shame, he soon came out as gay. Initially, he felt liberated from all of the secrecy as he focused on pursuing his own desires. What he found, though, wasn't very appealing. "I found out what a bad friend I was. I was unfaithful to my boyfriends, having one-night stands that left me feeling like, 'Ugh. I'm making a mess of my life.' I had this realization that, even though it felt liberating at first, I was still under the weight of so much guilt and shame from the choices I was making, and I didn't know how to make other ones."

One morning, Andrew woke up after a night of heavy partying only to realize that he'd tried to coerce someone into having sex with him the night before. Face to face with who he'd become, he thought to himself, *I wouldn't want to be my friend. I wouldn't want to be around me; I'm not safe.* At that moment, he opened his heart completely to the Lord and handed over the reins of his life. As he cried out to God, the mercy of Jesus washed over him and he heard God say, "Andrew, I'm not mad at you."

For the first time since he could remember, Andrew suddenly was free of guilt and shame. As soon as he chose to place himself vulnerably before the Lord, he was met by God's loving presence and His unending grace. The next step was to get vulnerable with some trustworthy people. "I got some good counseling and a good church environment. I saw that I could talk to God about anything. I didn't have to hide or get myself fixed to be pleasing to God. I could talk about my pain. I could talk to my friends at church about my pain and struggles, and I could get support when I needed it." This shifted everything about how he related to God, to other people, and to himself.

Soon, he didn't need to label himself as gay to make sense to the men around him. He realized that God had made him a man, and that was enough. And he began to open up his world to include other trustworthy people. "God used some older men and my friends who were guys to show me what it means to be a man. So, I started to feel comfortable in my skin as a man." Seven years after giving his life to Christ, he met and married an amazing woman with whom he now has four children. But his same-sex attraction didn't just disappear. "From time to time, same-sex attraction can still be a part of my life, but what has changed is that it doesn't have authority over me anymore. And, when I experience it, I know I can go back to God to ask what happened. Am I isolated right now, or do I have community? I can talk to God and then go back to my friends and say, 'This is what's going on. Will you pray for me?'" Andrew's process of vulnerability continually opens the door to quick restoration with God, within himself, and with his community. He finds this openness and lifestyle fulfilling and life-giving.[5]

It is choices like these that are the building blocks of a life lived in intimacy. God invites us to *"come boldly to the throne of grace"* (Hebrews 4:16). He is not angry, waiting for us to fail so that he can dole out punishment. He is on our side. He is applauding us as we take each step, waiting and ready to remove the sin and pain from our hearts and lead us into freedom. We get to take our worst selves before the throne of God, and He gently reminds us who we have been created to be. We get to stop being our own judge and jury, beating ourselves up with isolation and shame, and instead submit to the most gentle and empowering Father who invites us into a place of intimacy with Him and with others. He has made a space for us to lay down our guard, release control over our own lives, and receive His unconditional love. He has so much freedom waiting for us on the other side.

Questions to Ask Yourself

- Do the friends who champion you toward God's vision for your life truly know you—the real you? Do you let them know when you feel weak or are failing?

- What aspects of your life do you hide from your friends and family?

- Why do you hide those things, if you do, from the people who care about you?

- Is there any sin from your past or present life that you have never told anyone about? If so, how would it feel to share that with a trustworthy person and not be rejected but instead embraced by that person?

- What can you do to increase your vulnerability with trusted loved ones in your life?

Activations

- **The Hidden Things:** Spend some time with the Lord and ask Him why you have hidden certain areas of your life from your friends and family. Write down what He says.

- **Dr. Brené Brown on "The Power of Vulnerability":** Watch this video (20:49 in length) on YouTube. Take notes about what vulnerability is and what it offers.

- **Getting Current:** Purpose to become more vulnerable with and known by your loved ones. Review the description of ideal people to be vulnerable with in the "Out of Hiding" section of this chapter. Think through what aspects of yourself or your behavior you feel led to share and with whom. Make a definitive plan of when and where to meet with a certain person and share what you're feeling led to share. Then, ask them to pray for you and thank them for being someone you can trust. Finally, ask how they are doing, listen well, and demonstrate that you are a safe place for their vulnerability.

Notes

1. Brené Brown, "The Power of Vulnerability," YouTube video, 20:49, Posted by TED, January 3, 2011, https://www.youtube.com/watch?v=iCvmsMzlF7o.

2. Brené Brown, "Listening to Shame," YouTube video, 20:38, Posted by TED, March 16, 2012, https://www.youtube.com/watch?v=psN1DORYYV0

3. Kris Vallotton, "The Power of Authenticity," Online sermon, 18:00, BethelTV.

4. Carmen Vaught, *CHANGED: #oncegay Stories,* https://changedmovement.com/stories/carmen-vaught.

5. Testimony: Andrew Franklin, in discussion with CHANGED Movement staff, 2019.

Chapter 5

SURRENDER

While the concept of vulnerability has become more attractive recently, surrender is still anything but sexy. The image that comes to most people's minds is the waving of a white flag on the battlefield—defeated, beaten down, a loser. Our Western culture celebrates individuals fighting for their rights, their subjective definition of truth, and their freedom to identify based on feelings. In this postmodern era, we are surrounded by a culture that cheers on people's ability to create their own reality.

The problem is that this mindset doesn't bring fulfillment. Our human concepts of freedom and happiness can easily get skewed. While the world is promoting a version of solipsistic self-care, Jesus says that *"It is more blessed to give than to receive"* (Acts 20:35). God isn't just giving us a commandment; He is sharing with us the truth of our very design. We were deliberately created by our Father to be blessed when we give to others, to be the greatest version of ourselves when we engage with Him like little children, and to find true freedom when we follow Jesus' leadership rather than our own. Choosing to surrender to Jesus' ways will change everything.

But it is here—making the decision to surrender—where I most often see people stuck. To give up control of our lives can be legitimately terrifying, particularly if we haven't yet known God as a good Father. We can be tempted to cling to power, believing that we know better than God does about what we need. Isn't that just the angle the serpent took when he convinced Eve to take a bite of the forbidden fruit? The enemy constantly tries to tell us that trusting Jesus is dangerous, that we will miss out, that God is just trying to control us, and that we would be better off if left to our own devices. However, human history proves that this is a lie. God tells us to have no other gods before Him (see Exodus 20:3). We are to put nothing ahead of His dominion over our lives.

A Good, Good Father

These are not warm, fuzzy concepts. The Bible says that we are to offer our "*bodies a living sacrifice, holy, acceptable to God*" (Romans 12:1). We worship God with our minds, our emotions, and our bodies. These are our offerings—a serious matter. But the great news is that the One we are called to surrender to in this complete way is not of the same caliber as our bosses, our neighbors, or even our earthly parents. We can hand over the reins of our lives with confidence, trusting in God's goodness and faithfulness. He is the One behind the Good News. He says that His Kingdom is "*righteousness and peace and joy*" (Romans 14:17). He came up with Heaven and the garden of Eden. He's the One to whom we are surrendering our lives.

Well into my journey, I was meeting with Ken. On that night, he was praying, ministering to me, and leading me to pray along with him. Deeply engaged in this tender moment, I heard him shift gears and say to me, "OK now pray, 'I give up all of my rights to be gratified by a man sexually ever again.'"

I froze. I understood the words that he was saying, but I realized that I couldn't pray that. I was baffled. I had spent the last 15 years reading books on transformation, going through five years of weekly professional counseling, and two nine-month programs based on walking out of homosexuality. How could I have spent hundreds of hours going after this most important life issue and not be willing to give up my right to be sexually gratified by a man?

Realizing I couldn't honestly pray those words, I told Ken, "I'm sorry. I need the weekend to think that through."

Filled with affection for me after a year of working together, Ken just shook his head and laughed, "You're so messed up, Ken. All right, take your time."

I knew I had stumbled onto something important. Jesus was the Savior of my life, but He clearly wasn't yet the Lord of my life. And I knew that was a problem. I needed to actually consider what praying that prayer of surrender would mean. "What if I never had another orgasm? What if my attraction to men never subsided? What if I never had a fulfilling sexual relationship with a woman?" I had to lay these possibilities before me so that I could choose to surrender in my present reality, not choose to surrender only *if* God was going to come through for me in the way that I imagined.

As the weekend ended, though, I began to turn my focus on who I knew God to be. I realized that He had a pretty good track record of coming through for me in the areas of my life where I had really turned toward Him. Jesus died on the cross for my sins. Some of my choices had resulted in His absolute agony, and yet He still wanted to have a relationship with me. More than that, He loved me extravagantly. That next week, I prayed and soberly made a quality decision about my life. I wholeheartedly gave up all my rights to ever be sexually gratified by a male again. And, with that decision, I stepped into one of my greatest breakthroughs ever.

Without being aware of it, I had been holding on to some control over my sexuality, keeping it like a safety net in my back pocket. When I laid it all down at God's feet, I made up my mind in a new way. Scripture says that *"A double minded man is unstable in all of his ways"* (James 1:8 KJV). Suddenly, I was no longer unstable. I had set my stake in the ground. I had put all of my eggs in God's basket, and my mind was singularly focused on following Jesus. When temptation came, I didn't need to decide anything because I already had: Undressing men with my eyes hurt God's heart, so it wasn't an option. Porn was completely off-limits for me. Orgasm would never involve a male. I sacrificed those guilty pleasures for the joy of being able to rest and say, "All of my fulfillment is found in following Christ alone."

I gave up all my rights to sexual gratification, and He met me with more than I could have imagined. Bill Johnson says, "Fire falls on sacrifice." We lay our lives down at His feet, but we soon find out that we cannot out-give God. He is better than we are and more generous than we can imagine. We cannot choose to surrender in order to get something because often His return is different from what we had in mind. But it is always better, and He has eternity to reveal His generosity to us. James tells us, *"Therefore submit to God. Resist the devil and he will flee from you. Draw near to God and He will draw near to you. ...Humble yourselves in the sight of the Lord, and He will lift you up"* (James 4:7-10).

When we decide to deeply and genuinely surrender our will to God, the enemy—that accuser of the brethren who haunts us with perversion, lust, and pain—runs in terror from us. And the Lord—the intimate creator of our lives—draws close. He lifts us up higher than we could ever lift ourselves. Stop and think about that. Surrendering control of my sexuality completely changed my life.

Surrendering Harmful Behavior

When we choose to surrender our lives to Him, a part of that is surrendering the harmful behaviors that have restricted our ability to experience true intimacy with Him, with other people, and even with our own hearts. This process has to be done with the Holy Spirit because what God asks us to lay down is incredibly personal. Whether He invites us to discontinue certain activities forever or for just a season, He is all-knowing and works to answer our own prayers about our future. We must trust that Father God knows what we need.

The most obvious behavior to leave behind is any kind of sexual sin. Whether these are sexual acts with someone other than an opposite-sex spouse or looking to pornography to get our intimacy needs met, this behavior needs to stop. For those of us who are married, sexual sin can be particularly grievous because of the pain it causes our spouses. This behavior, along with any illegal activity whatsoever, must be addressed immediately. Honest confessions must be made and help—either from a pastor or a counselor—sought after. Doing so is a painful demonstration of surrender, but it is also the beginning of restoration and freedom. Sexual sin damages our ability to receive and give intimacy, and it can even harm our physical bodies, so it cannot remain in our lives. Thankfully, Romans 6 promises us freedom from the domination of sin, as we will discuss in Chapter 7.

Similarly, pornography acts as a mask to cover the true needs of our hearts. It has become so pervasive in our contemporary society that some Christians may even say that it's not a big deal, but that is a lie. Porn facilitates lust and, therefore, saddens the heart of God. It is incredibly destructive to the thought patterns in our minds, to our ability to relate to other people, and to our sex lives with our spouses. Extricating ourselves from sexual sin, for some, is a bumpy process. We need to remember that there is grace if we fall into sexual sin as we navigate this journey to wholeness. But we also need to be sober and realize that the enemy is working to destroy our lives with this sin. I tell people, "Treat sexual sin like cancer. Do everything you can to get rid of it. It's robbing you of the life God has for you." The trick, though, is how we address it. We must lean in close to the Holy Spirit, look to Him, and follow His lead. He will guide us away from sinful behavior when we are deeply surrendered and walking with Him.

Today, I can trust myself with a smartphone, but when I was in the midst of this battle I wasn't able to refrain from sinful behavior while having such easy access to the temptation that a smartphone offers. So God led me to remove the familiar objects of temptation from my life for a season to help me be more successful in my purity walk. And eventually, I grew in my ability to handle different freedoms. God has promised to direct our paths when we trust Him, so He will show us the things we need to lay down. It may be certain movies for one and all movies for another. Some people may need to surrender private time with their computer or even living alone, while other people may need to download a program like Covenant Eyes, which reports all of your computer's usage to pre-established accountability partners. Here's the thing: Continuing to stumble over temptations and indulge in sin significantly slows our journey toward freedom. So we need to obey the Lord and surrender whatever He asks us to surrender. He knows which things will cause us to compromise and which ones will not. He is committed to leading us into wholeness, and He knows how to get us there. This is easier to do when we are vulnerable with trusted people about our weaknesses and temptations and inform them of the things we're committing to surrender.

In this same way, we also want to take an honest look at any sort of addictive behavior, whether it is sexual or otherwise. If there is anything—alcohol, drugs, video games, masturbation, food, TV, or staring at a smartphone—that effectively numbs us from our present reality or masks pain, we can simply ask the Holy Spirit if He is wanting us to lay it down. Addictions are temporary medications, numbing agents that keep us from living fully—and from living fully aware. It may be daunting to let go of what has, in some ways, served as a comfort. We may feel there's no way we'll be able to cope without our crutch. But perfection is not the goal. God asks for humble hearts and our willingness to surrender and to follow (see James 4:1-10). He will be faithful to meet us with comfort, counsel, and breakthrough as we walk through this process. He will give us grace to follow His instruction. In scenarios like this, we need to request support, encouragement, and prayer from our trusted friends as well because they also can relay God's counsel and encouragement, leading us toward victory and freedom.

When the Lord invites us to surrender something to Him, it is for our protection. It is an opportunity for us to lay down our pride and to practice letting Him truly be the Lord over our lives. We can't expect to receive the promises of God—freedom, peace, righteousness, joy—if we don't follow Him. Obedience is the shortcut on this journey. It's that simple. We obey His leading, and then we get to experience the peace and breakthrough that come along with surrendering our lives to His leadership. He gave His life for our freedom, so we ought to position ourselves in such a way as to experience it.

If we're living our lives on our own terms most of the day and then hoping that God will show up for us in our moment of struggle, we've already lost. The secret is closeness—the kind of relationship with God that is all-consuming, where we never change the subject. My friend Drew Berryessa said, "I began to evaluate how I was living my life *in between* moments of overt sin. It was clear that there were habitual behaviors that consistently dulled my heart and sensitivity to the Lord and pulled my heart away from engaging with the Holy Spirit."[1] But as Drew became more sensitive to honoring the Lord's presence in the "in between" moments, focused himself back on the Lord, and proactively replaced negative behaviors with life-giving ones, the negative behaviors faded away. To the world, this kind of freedom from porn and sexual sin seems impossible. But with God and the community of people He has put in your life, all things are possible. *"It is for freedom that Christ has set us free"* (Galatians 5:1 NIV).

Surrendering Judgment

I'll bet every person who has battled same-sex attraction can identify with judgment. Many of us have heartbreaking tales of being judged by our peers and even by the adults in our lives who were supposed to protect us. This has a traumatizing effect on the hearts and minds of every individual, especially one who is wrestling at a fundamental level with personal identity. There is absolutely no excuse for the bullying, teasing, rejection, or emotional abuse that so many gay-identifying individuals have suffered. However, sometimes people who have been judged harshly can take on pride and judgment themselves as a protective barrier between their hearts and the people who might cause them pain.

I did this with men. As I described earlier, I felt insecure around my own biological sex; I was unable to fit in with the guys. So, as if to preempt the inevitable rejection from other men, I judged both the concepts of sexuality and masculinity as "less than." But when we make judgments like those, we are essentially kicking God off of the throne, declaring that our ideas about creation, about sexuality, and about the world are superior to His. Such an attitude is disrespectful and naïve. He is the Creator of the universe, and we are His creation. It behooves us to keep that in mind and lay our judgments at His feet.

However safe it feels to hide behind pride and scorn, hiding keeps us from fully submitting to God. Pride stands above others and looks down on their weaknesses, but surrendering to God is a work of humility. A true, deep, meaningful relationship with Him demands that we get on our knees and admit that we don't know what we're doing. It compels us to relinquish our rights to hold judgments about others, aligning our minds fully with God. Surrender means that we lay down our personal measuring rods, take Father God's hand, and let Him lead the way.

Surrendering to His Lordship

Elizabeth Woning and I have been working in ministry together for five years. She left a lesbian lifestyle and has walked out her surrender to God in an incredibly thoughtful way. She has allowed me to share her story along with her thoughts on this process:

> Throughout most of my life I never belonged. I always felt excluded, and I questioned my sexuality and my biological sex. I hated the idea of being feminine because it was so foreign. I didn't feel like a girl, but I also didn't identify as a boy.
>
> I made my first meaningful connection with another woman when I was in my mid-teens. We had such deep intimacy

> and love that our bond set a standard for my other relation-
> ships for several years. Though I occasionally dated men,
> and briefly in my early 20s was married to a man, I never
> developed fulfilling or lasting relationships with them.[2]

Her young marriage disintegrated, and she began to explore a homosexual lifestyle. Concluding that a homosexual identity explained feelings she had experienced in her childhood and young adulthood, she embraced lesbianism. As a part of the LGBTQ community, she found a powerful voice and new identity.

> I "came out" in my early twenties and moved to a mostly
> LGBTQ neighborhood in a metropolitan area. It was the
> culmination of years of internal questioning. Coming out
> in the '80s and '90s was a bold, public statement of iden-
> tity that took courage. Its losses in my life (in family and
> childhood relationships) felt balanced by gains, not least of
> which was the discovery I could belong and be accepted. I
> had a voice as a lesbian that was undaunted because I felt
> I had nothing left to lose. I was independent, powerful, but
> quietly heartbroken.
>
> Anyone who has left the familiar in order to "come out"
> knows surrender. One takes a leap of faith, with much risk,
> to publicly embrace an LGBTQ identity. Often, once accom-
> plished, bridges have been burned; high school reunions
> pose new dilemmas; and your childhood memories take
> on new meaning. You've changed your hair, your ward-
> robe, even your career. Before you know it, you are fully
> entrenched in rainbow covered Equality events and the
> upcoming drag queen competition.

God asks nothing less dramatic when He invites you to enter His life. His Kingdom. You are now a new creation: a son or daughter of God.

I met Jesus among a group of teenagers on a Thursday night. It was at a storefront Christian outreach for local teens. Nevermind that I was in my mid-thirties and had a Master's Degree in Theology. (I attended seminary openly lesbian.) My experience that night didn't fit in my neatly ordered intellectual picture of God's holiness. Instead, through the voice of a 17-year-old, God revealed that He knew me. Personally. That night's "word of knowledge" led me to a discovery process focusing on God's character that continues today. I recall thinking, *If God knows me individually, I have no idea who He really is.* I began a complete re-evaluation of my understanding of God. He didn't invite me to understand myself, but to discover Him, yet in that beautiful arrangement, I began to see myself differently. God began to reverse that misguided LGBTQ surrender in my life.

Compassionately, but persistently the Holy Spirit leads us to turn wholeheartedly to God. Every self-defined persona must be shed. This is one way that we express our love to Jesus (see John 14:15).

Surrender is one of the most important disciplines of my spiritual formation. It involves a powerful mixture of self-sacrifice with bold hope. I'm convinced God is eager for us to surrender the habits and mindsets that keep us from Him. Certainly our distorted perspectives regarding sexuality are among these hindrances (see 1 Thessalonians 4:3-8), but I wouldn't start there. Your self-perception

107

is a complex architectural construction comprised of childhood traumas, family experiences and cultural pressures that God will mysteriously reorder. Begin in prayer, asking God where to focus. I call that my "irresponsible look away." That is, turning my gaze away from myself to Him.

You may think to yourself, "I've prayed over and over that God would remove these feelings. He never has."

At some point, you will realize that God is exposing what you truly believe about Him and about yourself, and He is so convincing and compelling we find it easy to comply with His ideas.

Except when it isn't.

What is the belief you have about yourself that is painful to release? Or even humiliating to let go of? I recall being in that place when I discovered I was a woman. Yes, NOT a lesbian. The concession that I was "merely" a woman was fraught with struggle. Remember, lesbianism gave me a voice and belonging...and protection. I had NO vision for anything else. In fact, I didn't want what I feared God was inviting me into. We were at an impasse. It took great humility and courage to pick up God's vision for my life, which at the time I could only see as an empty page. I didn't know what should go on it, only that I trusted God would create something beautiful. He would be responsible for getting me there as long as I didn't erase what He was writing, or, worse, throw away the page. The hardship of surrender is that you can't be the author.

You have to release yourself completely from that thing He is highlighting before you will begin to see something new. If you somehow secretly hold on to gay identity, or the comfort of same-sex attraction, watching to see if God's way proves true, nothing will happen. "If my feelings never change, then it will have been true that I am gay," is not logic that can be applied before the Lord. God will respond with as much as you give. Faith is like currency. Just remember that God is love and He will delight you with the gift He has in store: a life you never thought could be possible.

My experience of God's love, the Christian community around me, and my desire to pursue a life of prayer had a dramatic influence on my life.

I came to terms with the impact misogyny had on my self-perception and pursued pastoral care and counseling that addressed childhood hurts and perceptions. Above all, I acknowledged I had rejected myself as a woman.

I did not specifically seek change in my sexuality; nevertheless, I began experiencing changes in my sexual desires. I became attracted to a man, which was one of the most unexpected and humiliating experiences of my life, since I had so fully identified as a lesbian. He and I got married and have had a strong marriage of 16 years thus far. Today I am happy, joyful, and feminine—all things that I never was while living as a lesbian. I am no longer sexually attracted to women. Rather, I am a strong advocate for their empowerment to overcome the effects of injustices against them.[3]

Elizabeth's life is an example of both the struggle to surrender and the incredible fruit of surrendering our lives to the One who made us. John writes:

> Listen carefully: Unless a grain of wheat is buried in the ground, dead to the world, it is never any more than a grain of wheat. But if it is buried, it sprouts and reproduces itself many times over. In the same way, anyone who holds on to life just as it is destroys that life. But if you let it go, reckless in your love, you'll have it forever, real and eternal (John 12:25 MSG).

Because of her surrender, Elizabeth was free to discover her true identity in Christ and to develop authentic, deep relationships with the people around her.

Questions to Ask Yourself

- Ask God if you hold any beliefs about yourself or your identity that He is inviting you to let go of or that you believe are contrary to His directives in the Bible. What are they?

- Ask God if you have formed in your mind negative judgments about yourself, God, or others. Have you formed negative judgments about sexuality, femininity, or masculinity? Write down each one.

- Ask God if there are any harmful or addictive behaviors the Lord is prompting you to surrender to Him. What are they?

- Have you given up all your rights to any kind of self-gratification or living life on your own terms? If not, ask God which "rights" you are hanging on to and write them down.

Activations

- **Renewing the Mind:** Review your answers to the questions above. Then, spend some time with the Lord asking His forgiveness and repenting for each of the attitudes, actions, beliefs, behaviors, and judgments that He invited you to address.

- **Total Surrender:** As I mentioned in Chapter 1, consider what, if anything, is in the way of your completely surrendering your entire life to His lordship. Consider what it will mean for you to lay everything down and give up all your rights to self-gratification or to living life on your own terms. Then, tell the Lord that you are surrendering completely to His lordship. Invite Him to direct every single area of your life for the rest of your life. Write down anything that the Lord reveals to you.

Notes

1. Drew Berryessa in *Finding You: An Identity-Based Journey Out of Homosexuality and Into All Things New* (2020).
2. Elizabeth Woning, *CHANGED: #oncegay Stories,* https://changedmovement.com/stories/elizabeth-woning.
3. Elizabeth Woning, "An Invitation to Surrender," *Finding You: An Identity-Based Journey Out of Homosexuality and Into All Things New* (2020).

Chapter 6

RELATIONSHIPS

The greatest commandment of the Bible is to *"love the Lord your God with all your heart"* (Matthew 22:37). We are called, first and foremost, to take the path of surrendering our will into God's loving hands. But the second greatest commandment that Jesus gives us is a relational one: *"You shall love your neighbor as yourself"* (Matthew 22:39). Our connection with one another—that we have it and how we do it—is of such vital importance to God that He lists it directly beneath our connection to Him.

Without relationships, life is devoid of meaning. This is why one of the highest forms of punishment in our correctional system in the U.S. is solitary confinement. The effects of this near complete isolation from human contact have been studied by psychologists, and the overarching conclusion is this: We were designed to live our fullest life in relationship with those around us.[1]

Great Pain, Great Healing

Relationships are a source of pain for every person alive. And for those of us who have dealt with same-sex attraction, connecting with others of the same sex can be complicated and even terrifying. It sounds illogical. The very people we feel difficulty connecting with and possibly even alienated or rejected by (the same sex) are the very ones we're desiring closeness (a sexual connection) with. Growing up, I had very few friendships with other boys my age. And the connections I did have often served to solidify my feelings of rejection and inadequacy. I had a deep longing to be able to fit in with the other males, though. In college, I joined an all-male, Christian fraternity and, for the first time, experienced what it was like to be one of the men and to live among them—which was, for me, both humiliating and deeply affirming. So, as I became more comfortable with my vulnerability and surrendered my heart to God's leading, I knew I needed to further press into relationships.

We are not born knowing how to connect with one another in a healthy way. We are taught by our families and our personal experiences how to relate to one another. I've found that for most people with same-sex attraction, that process of learning how to connect deeply with people of our own biological sex was somehow disrupted, confused. This is not a point of shame, but it does mean that we need to re-learn how to do healthy relationships. There is an aspect of healing that God intentionally places for us in community. Something comes alive within our hearts when we get connection and affirmation from people who are our same biological sex.

Relationships in general may have felt like a minefield, but God longs to teach us the steps we need to forge strong, healthy, life-giving connections with others. It is never too late to humble ourselves, get curious about the people around us, and establish those healthy connections.

We are the Body of Christ. Jesus taught us to pray, "*Our Father in Heaven*," not "My Father" (Matthew 6:9). If we push past the discomfort and fear of the unknown, restoration can be found in relationship with others. Other people may have been a great source of pain for many of us, but they will also be a great source of healing if we allow them. This is the reality that my friend Rodger Gaskin discovered as he pressed into the discomfort of bonding with other men in his journey toward wholeness.

I was born "that way," or at least that is the way it felt. For most of my life I was only sexually attracted to men. While I longed for both emotional and sexual intimacy with a man, I also felt as though I didn't belong with other men and that I was a foreigner. At the same time, most of my life I have been surrounded by men who valued and pursued non-sexual relationships with me. They didn't see me as an outsider or as less than. Many of them knew I struggled with homosexuality, but this didn't deter them from caring for me. Yet I couldn't connect with them. I was deeply uncomfortable with them while longing to be with them.

In my 20s, I started to explore ways to better integrate my faith and sexuality. I began reading books on the topic, and I attended a conference for people with unwanted sexual attractions. I saw a therapist and worked on many issues, including childhood trauma and depression. And I spent time, often at these conferences or other gatherings, with men and women who had experienced significant change in their sexual orientation.

These resources gave me a vision and hope that real change was possible and that it wasn't a fraudulent claim. At the core of all of this has been a belief that God's power is real and active today. With this, I have a personal commitment to the belief that sexual relationships are intended to be expressed between a man and a woman only.

At this point in my life, I have experienced magnificent change in the quality of my life. The greatest change has been in how I relate to other men. While I previously felt like an outsider and like I didn't belong, I am now very comfortable in my relationships with other men. Amazingly, I also find myself sexually attracted to women; what an oddly wonderful experience. With this, there has been a change in my sexual attraction toward men. The more comfortable and closer I have come relationally with other men, the less sexual attraction I have for men.

As I have addressed areas of confusion, trauma, and fear, the power of homosexual desire has lessened. My attention has gone from dealing with the attraction itself to dealing with the root issues behind it. The overall quality of my life has improved, and I am confident and secure in who I am as a human who is fully male. I continue to grow as a man and as a follower of Jesus.[2]

Father God

We were born into a family, even if our natural family was absent or divided. We were never meant to be islands. As we begin to create healthy relationships and expand our relational capacity, many of us will need to lay down the pride of self-sufficiency so that we can integrate into relationships in a healthy way.

God's value for relationship is modeled at the most foundational level in the trinity: He is God the Father, the Son, and the Holy Spirit. This is an inextricable relationship at the very heart of our faith. If God is the Father, He is the Father of every one of us. This journey can often look like connecting to our heavenly family, receiving our identities as sons and daughters of God. He created us in our mothers' wombs (see Psalm 139:13). He knew us before we were ever conceived (see Psalm 139:16). He no longer calls us servants, but friends (see John 15:15) and not only friends, but His children and co-heirs with His Son (see Romans 8:17).

Nothing has been as transformative in my life as the revelation that God is not only all-powerful, all-knowing, and ever-present—He is relational. He is God the Father, God *my* Father. As Christians, many of us can serve God with our whole hearts for our entire lives without truly recognizing the attentive fathering that He brings into our lives. The enemy works hard to distract us from this truth, to make us believe we are alone, without provision, forced to define our own identities. But we each have a tender, loving Father. And it is only through Him that we can understand our true identities.

Many of us have lived our whole lives feeling like orphans. This can be a source of deep pain, especially if we are living with our natural families. But God wants us to experience Him as our loving Father who delights in us, takes care of us, has a plan for our lives, and will be with us forever. Embracing this heavenly family—God the Father, Christ His Son, and the Holy Spirit—as our own and as one that God has designed for us to participate in is the beginning of this shift. Much transformation comes from leaning into God as our Father. The apostle John laid his head on Jesus' chest. So should we.

Mom and Dad

In addition to our heavenly family, our earthly family also plays a big part in our pursuit of building healthy relationships. If there is abuse or other destructive behavior, this advice will likely not apply and pursuit of a parental relationship would not be advised. Follow the Holy Spirit's leading either way. But for many of us, pressing into our families of origin can bring significant breakthrough. We don't want to let pain from the past stand as a roadblock to our connections with our parents. God is the one who puts us into family, so we can trust that the Holy Spirit will guide us in our reconnection. God tells us, *"Honor your father and your mother"* (Exodus 20:12). He wouldn't command it if it was going to be easy all of the time, but, because He commands it, we know that it is possible. And we know the benefit: *"that your days may be long upon the land which the Lord your God is giving you"* (Exodus 20:12). There can be a life-giving connection in our family bonds, and we can be the ones to make the first step of moving toward our parents with vulnerability, honesty, and curiosity instead of judgment.

Many struggling with same-sex attraction have bonded particularly with one parent over the other. For me, this was my mom. As soon as I came home from school, I would pour out the details of my day to my mom. My dad would've loved to have heard my thoughts and emotions about school. By the time he got home, though, I didn't feel the pressing need to share. And so, our relationship didn't grow in the same way. Things changed when I began to be more intentional with him as I matured. I began to save most of my verbal processing for when he was home. I began to ask him questions about his life. It was awkward at first, but soon our relationship strengthened and grew. Eventually, I felt as if he'd rather be spending time with me than any other person. So I chose him to be best man in my wedding. My dad is in Heaven now, and I am beyond grateful that we invested in our relationship and shared so many great years.

Many of us did not experience the parenting that our hearts needed. Only God is the perfect Father, so a part of this journey is allowing ourselves to be reparented. This can happen in our relationship with God, with our own parents, or even with spiritual parents and mentors. The Lord put several people in my life who poured into me as spiritual parents. They loved me, encouraged me, and invested in me as a man. But they also held me accountable for my growth and spoke the truth even when it was hard to hear. I had prayed for spiritual parents, and God gave me the right people for the right seasons of my life. It was up to me, though, to lean into those relationships.

Band of Brothers

Finally, as we pursue relationships within the context of family, we also need to learn the value of developing a band of brothers (or sisters). When I was just beginning to step out into vulnerability, I shared my journey first with close women friends. I was new at sharing deeply in that way and, in my mind, women were better listeners, better talkers, and more empathetic than their male counterparts. So I opened up to my cousin Amy, a friend of my mom's, and some ladies at my college. And that worked. It was a valuable step for me to begin allowing other people to truly see me, to feel their acceptance and love, and to build bridges back to healthy relationships. But I needed to heal my relationships with other men, and my counselor at the time saw that.

When he first recommended that I join a fraternity at my college, I was horrified. I was adamantly opposed to this idea. The thought of being in a locker room or dormitory with a bunch of guys or stuck at a men's retreat with no women to talk to was, at the time, my own version of hell. "Plus, weren't frats institutions of the devil?" I soon found a Christian fraternity, though, and was accepted as a member of a great group of young men. I was still terrified, but the Lord was being very intentional, and my hunger for freedom was genuine.

One day, most of the guys were out behind our fraternity house having a contest to see who could sink the most baskets. I felt frustrated, realizing that it was my fear that kept me from joining in. I had zero basketball skills, so I knew this activity wouldn't raise my esteem in their eyes. I was almost certainly going to be mocked mercilessly if I tried to make those shots. But I realized that even if I wasn't good, at least I was trying. So I stepped up to join the game. Miracle of all miracles, I picked up the basketball and—one after another—kept sinking my shots. Probably a dozen or more. A far better performance than most of the guys. I couldn't believe it! God met my feeble attempts with His grace, and there I was—feeling like the unathletic "gay" guy—getting cheered on by a crowd of rowdy young men.

The affirmation from other men did something profound in my heart that day. But I would never have experienced it had I not stepped out of my comfort zone and leaned into relationship with my newly forming band of brothers. And over the next years, I bonded deeply with six or seven of those men. They helped shape me—iron sharpening iron—with their attention and conversation. Their continued presence in my life showed me that I was a man, like them. I was a man worthy of their time. While they occasionally teased me for my sometimes less-than-masculine (stereotypically speaking) behaviors, they didn't file me in a separate category. I was one of them. At times they even defended me from others. And when I was humble enough to accept their input, they actually made me better. Thirty years later and thousands of miles apart, we still talk regularly and get together when we can. Their relationships have been vital.

Choosing Forgiveness

As we move toward the relationships that the Lord has intentionally placed in our lives, we must also be willing to shift some things in our own hearts to create a healthy atmosphere for connection. For those of us who have struggled with same-sex attraction, two of the most foundational shifts we often need to make include walking out forgiveness and developing emotionally healthy relationships. These both won't apply to the same degree for everyone, but, as we move along in this pursuit of wholeness, both releasing people from past offenses and learning to manage our own emotional needs in a healthy way will open the door to the potential for deep and lasting relationships.

Forgiveness is at the very heart of our walk with Jesus, and it is a crucial aspect in our connection with others. It's unreasonable to imagine that we could have thriving relationships with other people without experiencing hurt or offense occasionally. What we do with that pain, however, will determine the depth and health of our relationships and the fulfillment we receive from them.

When we have spent years feeling unloved, orphaned, or rejected by others, forgiveness can feel like a bitter pill to swallow. People can do horrible things to one another. Forgiving others for their negative impact on our lives does not mean that we are brushing off the pain, minimizing their actions, or even opening ourselves up to trusting those persons again. It simply means that we have taken the thorn of bitterness—the lie that says that we'll be able to get justice for

121

ourselves—and laid it down at the feet of Jesus. Like the saying goes, unforgiveness is like drinking poison and expecting the other person to die. Forgiveness neutralizes that poison, allowing your heart to receive the compassion and mercy of Christ.

Forgiveness has never been about whether the person deserves to be forgiven. Jesus cleared that up for us when He went to the cross for us *"while we were still sinners"* (Romans 5:8). In the midst of our mess, knowing that we would continue to go on sinning, He laid down His life for us. Seeing in advance every mistake we would ever make, He chose to endure unimaginable pain in order to wipe out every sin, and He called us His own.

Colossians 3:13 makes it clear that we must forgive others. It tells us that we must bear with one another *"forgiving one another, if anyone has a complaint against another; even as Christ forgave you, so you also must do."* We must follow Jesus' model and make the choice to forgive and bless those who have hurt us, releasing them entirely.

Breaking Codependency

My personal experience of same-sex attraction came with a heavy dose of codependency. I touched on this in my story toward the beginning of the book. I would fixate on a particular boy and become very dependent on him for identity, affirmation, and assurance. I'm not a psychologist, but my observation is that codependency is like human worship—worshiping another person—at least that's what it felt like to me. Whoever I was captivated by at the moment appeared perfect to me, and I began to idolize him. My entire life would be wrapped up in wondering about his opinions, considering how he would think about me in any given scenario. Sometimes, I wasn't even able to say what I thought about something until I processed it through the imagined mind of the other boy. It was actually an extreme version of self-loathing. In the worst seasons, I wanted to erase myself completely and replace myself with someone "better."

Not everyone's journey will be like this or will be this extreme. But codependency is not uncommon among people who struggle with same-sex attraction. As we've talked about before, because there is an unmet need for genuine intimacy, often fantasy or a kind of human worship tries to fill that emotional vacancy. It can manifest as a fixation on another person, a lack of peace unless that person is around, a deep need for an individual's attention and affirmation, or a jealous hunger for that person's uninterrupted presence that can eventually manifest as sexual desire.

In my case, my emotional need for masculinity in my life developed into an obsession with another male who seemed more perfect than my flawed self. As I journeyed on my own road to wholeness, I discovered what I was doing was a type of idolatry. Idols can take all different forms; they don't have to be small statues, sitting on a shelf. My need for identity, connection, and affirmation was so great that I had become more concerned with pleasing these boys/men than I was with pleasing God. Far more.

Breaking this cycle was, honestly, one of the hardest things I've ever had to do. It was breaking an all-consuming addiction, but it was one that actually opened up my life to getting the hunger of my heart truly satiated. I had to repent—for my obsession, for my lust, for my self-hatred, for my own manipulation, for the soulish bonds that I had developed with these boys/men—and I had to trust that God had a freedom for me that was more fulfilling than my addiction to other people. I had to receive the empowerment of God's grace and step into a totally new way of relating to people. And in a couple of specific cases, I had to completely break the relational connection I had with a guy I felt I was in love with. It was like experiencing the death of a very close loved one. I wouldn't wish it on anybody.

But because I allowed the Lord to free me from that kind of bondage, I now get to love my wife from a place of overflow. I don't come to her desperate to get my emotional needs met. I don't hate myself and want to replace myself with her. My heart knows how to receive intimacy. I have learned to walk in vulnerability, completely surrendered to the Lord, and the health of my relationships is the evidence. I don't worship my wife; she doesn't have to bear the weight of being my savior. I worship God and, from that intimate place of connection with Him, my love overflows onto her. I love who she is, I think she's incredibly beautiful, we connect deeply on multiple levels, and we have so much fun together. I don't need her to fix me. She is free to be herself with me, and I with her.

Building Healthy Community

That is the freedom we get to bring into our developing relationships. We get to approach trustworthy people with vulnerability, sharing our pain and our victories with them regularly. We get to be easy forgivers, releasing others from our judgment and instead offering the compassion that we receive from Christ. Learning to connect with others in a genuine, healthy way does not come easily. Relationships are work. They require a mutual give and take, an ability to communicate our inner worlds, and a willingness to listen with empathy to another's story. Deep relationships require a kind of trust that can only be built over time.

But they are so worth it. My encounters with God transformed my heart and mind, and my relationships changed my life. I can honestly say that I was fathered into wholeness. Hugh Cunningham, a pastor friend of mine, spent a couple of hours of his free time, week after week, listening to me pour out my heart on Saturday mornings. I felt his value for me. He would listen and listen to me. And he would deeply care and have empathy for my pain. And then he would feed back to me what he heard and saw and what the Lord was saying about me. He would affirm my masculinity and my sonship in God. He would expect me to live as the saint that God had made me to be.

One morning, I told him about another slip up with porn that I'd had. He kindly let me know that, if I looked at porn again, he would help me by taking my computer to his house where it would remain. Because we had built a deep relationship, rather than feeling controlled or condemned I felt loved. I felt the freedom of being held accountable to a tender father figure who was on my team. As it turned out, I peeked briefly at porn one last time and quickly notified him. He told me that was my last warning, and I knew he meant it. And I never looked at porn again.

It was crucial for me to find a community of Spirit-led believers. In an environment where God's Spirit was moving supernaturally, I was surrounded by people who followed the guidance of the Holy Spirit, who had seen the Lord move miraculously in people's lives, and who knew that He wanted to transform my life. All kinds of beneficial, random ministry moments happen there: words of divine wisdom, a word of encouragement, or the experience of being loved by others. My growth was significantly impacted by my environment. I was discipled by Jesus among a community of Jesus-lovers who had faith that God would show up and meet people's needs. Being regularly seen by people who truly know us and hear God on our behalf is foundational.

For many, the fact that God wants to speak to us is a new concept. But it's not anything new for Scripture. Jesus said, *"My sheep hear My voice, and I know them, and they follow Me"* (John 10:27). God promises that He will speak to us. None of us hear God perfectly, but He wants us to hear Him for ourselves and follow Him. He also invites us to hear His voice for others (see 1 Corinthians 12). There were so many times I was directed, encouraged, or healed by friends and leaders saying, "You know, Ken, the Lord laid this on my heart for you..." or "Ken, the Lord is inviting you to let go of fear." Also, allowing Him to speak to us—through dreams, visions, heavenly experiences, signs and wonders—can be vital to following His guidance into all truth; these are ways He speaks.

It is so important that we surround ourselves with a community of believers who hear God's voice and live with an awareness of the realities of the spirit realm. Spiritual warfare is very real even though we cannot see it with our natural eyes (see Ephesians 6:10-20). Throughout my journey, I've had to untangle which thoughts were my own and which thoughts were demonic torment. Because I had Spirit-led leaders, I was able to go through powerful times of deliverance and supernatural ministry that resulted in new levels of freedom that I could not have received on my own. The struggle with same-sex attraction is deeply complex. I am not advocating a "pray the gay away" kind of ministry. There are relational dynamics to shift, traumas to heal, and mindsets that need to be transformed (letting go of lies and grabbing hold of truth), but there is also a very real spiritual fight. And being a part of a Spirit-led community will make all the difference.

We find our true selves within community. It is only in the context of genuine friendship that we can hear the truth spoken in love, rubbing off the rough edges of our lives. When we allow ourselves to be truly seen and known, we are able to see God's nature reflected back to us in unique ways through each person. When we can press through the fear of relating to our same sex, we will find that we are much more alike than the enemy or our history may want us to believe. All of these benefits are by God's design. He created us to live in community, and it is there that we will experience our freedom and discover the fullness of our identities.

Questions to Ask Yourself

- Do you feel that you have a relationship with God such that you are aware of His fathering presence in your life? If not, what is keeping you from seeing God this way?

- Do you feel close to (deeply known by) your family members, particularly your same-sex parent/grandparents and siblings? Why or why not?

- Do you have any close, same-sex friends (your approximate age or older) who know you well and cheer you on to keep your eyes on Jesus? What did you learn from this chapter that can help you deepen your relationships with these friends?

- Do you have any mentors or "spiritual parents" championing you toward God's best for your life who know you deeply, see you frequently, and consistently speak into your life? Have you shared your sexual struggle with them? What, in general, has their main counsel been to you?

- Are you experiencing any fixation or emotional dependency on another person similar to what I described in the

"Breaking Codependency" section of this chapter? If so, which person(s) have you been fixated on?

Activations

- **Knowing God as Father:** Read Luke 15:11-32 with an awareness that God loves you as much as the prodigal son's father loved him. Meditate on the passage and ask the Lord what it means for you. Invite Father God to be your father and to father you. Take a moment and imagine Him showing you fatherly love and affirmation.

- **Band of Brothers/Sisters:** Make a plan for how you can create a band of brothers (if you're male) or sisters (if you're female) around yourself. These relationships could be with a same-sex parent/grandparents, mentors, siblings, relatives, and friends. The point is to proactively work to ensure you have five or more people who know you inside and out, who connect with you regularly and can help you mature in the Lord.

- **Forgiving Others**: Ask God to show you the people from your past who have hurt you. Write them down. Individually, ask God to give you compassion for each person and to allow you to see each person as He sees them. Think about how Jesus forgave you for your sins, though you didn't deserve to be forgiven. Then, talk to God and specifically declare your forgiveness for each person for the specific ways that they hurt you. Jason Vallotton's book *Winning the War Within* is a great resource on the topic of forgiveness.

- **Codependency:** If you have an emotional dependency upon another person, tell several of your trusted loved ones. Ask them to help you make a plan to separate from this person and to hold you accountable for doing so. Ensure that you are sharing your life with multiple loved ones to avoid creating a new fixation. The book *Codependent No More* by Melody Beattie may be helpful.

Notes

1. Elena Blanco-Suarez, Ph.D. "The Effects of Solitary Confinement on the Brain," *Psychology Today*, February 27, 2019, https://www.psychologytoday.com/us/blog/brain-chemistry/201902/the-effects-solitary-confinement-the-brain.
2. Rodger Gaskin, *CHANGED: #oncegay Stories,* https://changedmovement.com/stories/rodger-gaskin.

Chapter 7

IDENTITY

I was around 12 years old when, sitting on my bed reading the Bible, I came across this verse: *"Do you not know that the unrighteous will not inherit the kingdom of God? Do not be deceived. Neither fornicators, nor idolaters, nor adulterers, nor homosexuals, nor sodomites, nor thieves, nor covetous, nor drunkards, nor revilers, nor extortioners will inherit the kingdom of God"* (1 Corinthians 6:9-10). I panicked. As I read through the list, I had measured myself against the prohibited behaviors. I didn't worship idols (check), or practice adultery (check), or drink too much (check), or steal (check). But when I read about homosexuals, fear shot through my entire body. I thought, *If I'm being completely honest with myself, I'm not at all sexually attracted to girls, but I am attracted to guys.* And I'd just read that people like that—people like me—go to hell.

That was a terrifying thought to navigate all by myself at that age. Especially in that moment in time. Society wasn't like it is today. Ellen DeGeneres hadn't kissed a woman on TV yet. There was no movement declaring that homosexuality was a great option for an identity. This was the mid '80s. I was alone, afraid, and—apparently—detestable. God's Word said that what I was feeling was not OK. And there were other damning Scriptures. I sank deeper into despair as I found other verses that described homosexuality as a vile passion (see Romans

1:26), an abomination (see Leviticus 18:22), whose practitioners are unholy and profane (see 1 Timothy 1:9-10).

And as I've mentioned, there were no conversations in my church about transformation. I didn't yet have a grid for a God who would meet us in our places of need and change our lives Himself to conform to His standards for righteousness. My relationship with God was mostly fire insurance. If I punched the spiritual clock each week—reading my Bible daily, attending church plus the mid-week prayer meetings if I wanted extra credit—then Heaven was my reward. And now, even that was on the line.

For people facing areas of repetitive sin in their lives, this kind of religion does not satisfy. For years, I suffered in cycles of despair, hopelessness, and addictive self-soothing. It wasn't until I got to ministry school that my mind began to be transformed about who I was in Christ. See, in the midst of my panic, I'd never actually finished reading that passage from First Corinthians. Paul is addressing a community of believers dealing with immoral behavior. He lists examples of ungodly conduct, and that is where my brain had frozen. But in the very next verse, he concludes his thoughts. *"And such **were** some of you. But you were washed, but you were sanctified, but you were justified in the name of the Lord Jesus and by the Spirit of our God"* (1 Corinthians 6:11, emphasis added). Paul was writing this letter to people who used to be idolaters, adulterers, homosexuals, and thieves. But when they came to Christ, their lives changed. He wasn't condemning people to hell by listing those behaviors; he was reminding the Corinthians of their new identity in Christ.

A New Creation

For those of us walking out of a homosexual background, the enemy would love nothing more than to convince us that the things we are tempted by define us. But nowhere in the Bible is homosexuality understood to be an identity. It is a behavior, a choice of action that leaves us feeling disconnected from God, from our community, and from ourselves like every other sin. In fact, it is only in recent history that people have viewed homosexuality as innate or a possible identity. That is not surprising, considering the overall breakdown of sexual identity in our contemporary culture. Under the guise of throwing off prudish, old-fashioned restraints, the gifts of masculinity and femininity—with their diverse strengths and perspectives—have been stripped away. Instead, the "sexual revolution" has left behind confusion about sexual identity as a whole.

Homosexuality as a behavior, however, has been present throughout human history. But throughout Scripture, Jesus directs the river of our humanity by giving us healthy banks through which to flow. Knowing us better than we know ourselves, understanding what brings us life and what behavior slowly kills us, He sets parameters around the human expression. He shows us, by example, what a life lived in union with God looks like. We are not defined by what tempts us; we are defined by the One who created us. And He enables us to live victoriously in union with Him. He says, in fact, *"we are more than conquerors through him who loved us"* (Romans 8:37 NIV).

This act of redefining ourselves as children of God is a radical one. For Janet Boynes, it was what set her free. Now an ordained pastor, she wrestled with her identity for years before encountering God.

The trauma and pain from my childhood, which was filled with physical and sexual abuse, led me into a series of broken lesbian relationships. Before I entered into a lesbian lifestyle, I had been a Christian and was engaged to be married to a man. My fiancé was gone a lot, and I hated being alone, so I spent a lot of time with a woman from work. This interaction opened the door to my first sexual encounter with a woman, leading me away from God and my fiancé and into a life of lesbianism for 14 years.

Each time I tried to return to God, I felt pulled to hold on to that lifestyle. I even toyed with the idea of getting a sex change to make the relationships more "normal" but couldn't bring myself to go through with it. I became so miserable that I started looking for other ways to fill the void in my soul, including drugs and eventually bulimia.

One October morning in a grocery store I encountered a woman who invited me to her church. I knew right then and there that our meeting was not a coincidence and that this was a new beginning for me. Through this encounter in 1998, God intervened in my life and called me out of the lesbian lifestyle. With the help of people at my church in Minnesota, I never looked back. I had finally found what I was looking for. After living a lesbian lifestyle for 14 years, I found freedom through Jesus Christ.[1]

When we come to Christ, we participate both in His death and in His resurrection. We are born again—our old man falls away and, in its place, a new creation stands. When I first arrived at ministry school, I wanted to itemize every bad thing I'd ever done and share it with the leader of the school. The teaching was focused on receiving God's love and living out our identities as sons or daughters of God and co-heirs with Christ. But I wanted to make sure the leader knew every sin I had committed before evaluating whether or not I was worthy enough to receive that kind of acceptance. Lovingly, he teased me, pointing out that I was getting a bit stuck in my own head. He wasn't discounting my intellect, but he was guiding me to a greater reality. No matter what I had done, no matter how I had messed up, the Father's love for me was vast and steadfast. God knew me—truly saw me—and He loved me completely.

Receiving this love changed my life. I began to understand that there was more to life than living out this rigid algorithm of religion. I thought I was supposed to be stepping through a variety of hoops, punching the correct keys into God's computer program in order to be loved and accepted. Suddenly, I saw that God meant for me to be fully alive, and He wanted to show me how that would happen. God's desire was that I'd be comfortable in my own skin, navigating life from the security of His loving approval. The summer after that first year of ministry school, I spent hours each day in the campus prayer chapel. Over and over again, I read Romans 5–8. It began to sink in that God's love had chased me down in the midst of my shame-filled, sinful state. He wasn't repulsed by me. He was pursuing me, covering me with His grace, and inviting me to live as a completely new man.

Jesus chose to die for each one of us. And when we come to Christ, we retroactively participate in His death and resurrection. Who we were without Him dies—completely. Paul says that *"our old man was crucified with **Him**, that the body of sin might be done away with, that we should no longer be slaves of sin"* (Romans 6:6, emphasis added). And our new, cleansed beings—our new selves—rise with Christ so that we can reckon ourselves *"to be dead indeed to sin, but alive to God in Christ Jesus our Lord"* (Romans 6:11). We have died and are reborn. The shift starts in our minds and then—as a result of that—the old habits and sins no longer have a hold over us. Paul tells us to "reckon" ourselves to be dead to sin—believe in the transformative power of the cross—and that belief will begin to affect our behavior.

This doesn't mean that it is impossible for us to sin. In his book *Spirit Wars*, Kris Vallotton brilliantly points out that one doesn't need a "sin nature" to sin. Adam and Eve were the perfect example of this, living in the garden of Eden in a perfect environment. Kris says, "all you need to sin is a free will and the capacity to believe a lie. All believers possess these qualities."[2] We can withdraw from our new identity and act in discordance with who we are, but it is unnatural for us to do.

Once we belong to Christ, once His blood washes us clean, it is no longer in our nature to sin. Our DNA reflects our heavenly Father. Like the prodigal son, we have been given the robes of royalty, the dust of our old life has been wiped off of our records, and we have been adorned with our identity as God's kids. We are saints—slaves to righteousness (see Romans 6:18). But Kris taught me if I believe I'm a sinner, I will continue to sin. "You'll sin by faith," he likes to say. Kris says, "This is why John teaches us to believe that we will not sin as we learn to abide in Christ. He writes, 'No one who abides in Him sins; no one who sins has seen Him or knows Him.... No one who is born of God practices sin, because His seed abides in him; and he cannot sin, because he is born of God' (1 John 3:6-9 NASB)."[3]

I can't make the point strongly enough: What we believe about our identity has everything to do with what we will experience. If we believe that we are "gay" and that we can't help but experience that world of temptation, attraction, and behavior, that is what we will experience. But we don't have to accept an alt-identity. We who are being discipled by Christ have been given a new nature. We are no longer who we once were. We experience some temptation because we live in a realm (as Adam and Eve did) where we can hear from and be influenced by the devil and his minions who are, in fact, sinful. But if we will embrace our new-creation identities in Christ and reject the enemy's lies and efforts to convince us we are "gay" or any other untrue identity, we'll act in accordance. This is why I spent an entire summer meditating on these biblical truths. And it completely changed my life.

Owning Our Biological Sex

As our awareness of our new identity in Christ grows, as we begin to experience His love and acceptance, we can begin to embrace how He made us. A large part of this journey for those of us who have struggled with same-sex attraction is learning to come to terms with our own maleness or femaleness. Each one of us was born either as a male or a female. Chromosomally, this is a biological fact which is established at conception.[4,5] Scientifically, there is no other sexual identity option, no third sex. Sex chromosomes, gonads, and sex hormones bear this out.[6] Of course, there can be birth defects, or deformities that occur, such as disorders of sexual development (DSD). But DSDs ("intersex" is the informal term) are identifiable medical problems, and not rightly identities.[7] You have a DSD rather than being one. Obviously, the rare few who do have such birth defects may have significant challenges—biologically, emotionally, and socially—which inspire deep compassion.

Put another way, birth defects in a developing embryo might cause a child to be born without a limb. But as I was taught by my learned friend Dr. Andre Van Mol, a person well studied on the intersection of biology and homosexuality, this anomaly does not get to redefine the reality that humans were designed with two arms and two legs. Biological anomalies do not disprove or undercut what is normal. Sexual identity is similarly hardwired into our beings. Chromosomal abnormalities can occur, but, despite this, sexual identity is still either male or female. There is no alternate sexual identity beyond male or female.

Our male and female sexual identities are written into trillions of cells in our bodies. They are not restricted to our reproductive organs but influence every aspect of our beings at a cellular level.[8] For most of us struggling with same-sex attraction, though, identifying with our own biological sex can feel like a minefield of doubts, insecurities, and potential alienation. As I pointed out in Chapter 6, reclaiming our connection with people of our own biological sex in a non-sexualized way is crucial to our journey to wholeness. Rodger Gaskin describes his journey this way:

> One of the most powerful realities that has propelled me toward change is the truth that I am a new creation. For the majority of my Christian experience I didn't understand what this meant. While I believed that I was saved, I had no idea how powerful my salvation is. Because of this, I had little expectation or faith that I could experience change regarding same-sex attraction (SSA). I didn't realize that when I came to Christ I became a new person: I had a new identity. I was set free from the old self and now as a new creation in Jesus I was putting on a new self.
>
> I also had to embrace my gender, which is inextricably intertwined with my biological sex. This can be humbling, offensive and fear provoking. I felt like I didn't fit in, like I didn't have my "man card." So, I refused to engage in "manly" activities. To my chagrin, God began bringing manly men

around me. They pursued friendship with me, inviting me to go shooting, hunting, fishing, play sports, and help with building projects. While I searched for reasons to refuse their offers, my resistance was actually masking fear. The truth is that I was just embarrassed at my lack of ability or experience with those settings and activities. A friend told me that I needed to push through my fears and engage men in these ways. I can tell you many stories that would make you laugh, but the outcome of my pressing through fear is a growing comfort and self-awareness of being masculine. Now when I'm with men, I know I belong.

Jesus' Gospel powerfully saves and transforms us as we trust and engage Him. My God-designed identity as a man and a follower of Christ continues to unfold/solidify/become clear the more I pursue Him. My sexuality and biological sex are always within the reaches of His transforming power. I am a new creation.[9]

Though I believe God can do anything, finding this kind of comfort and confidence in our own biological sex may not often happen overnight. Early in my journey, even the idea of walking past the men's locker room used to give me anxiety. The first times I pressed into relationships with other men, it felt awkward and terrifying. That's OK. Transformation does not need to be immediate. We can't expect to put a hunting rifle or a baseball bat into the hands of a guy who has felt alienated from other men his entire life and expect him to be suddenly comfortable with his masculinity. It's not that simple. And rifles and bats aren't the sum total of masculinity, anyway.

Owning our sexual identities can be a process, but one that the Lord has fully equipped us to emerge from victoriously. God isn't asking you to put on a show. He created you as a man or a woman, and that is enough. Change doesn't come by our efforts to *prove* our biological sex to anyone. However, leaning into our biological sex, being willing to connect and adjust a few of our behaviors, is a life-giving and transformational part of fully claiming and experiencing our God-given identities. We can press into owning our biological sex or not. In many seasons I did not. But we have a God who calls us by name, who gives true identity in Him, and who empowers us with the grace to embrace those true identities.

Our job is to place our focus on hearing His voice. We don't need to fake our transformation. That doesn't work anyway. Such efforts only lead to shame and humiliation. Rather, our focus can rest fully on investing in our intimate relationship with God and with the people (particularly people of the same sex) He has placed in our lives. Doing this enables us to fully embrace all aspects of our biological sex instead of being limited by insecurities, which compel us to opt out of or restrict parts of our identity. This is a predominantly internal battle, but one that God is fully capable of helping us navigate. My friend KathyGrace Duncan took testosterone, had surgery to remove her breasts, and lived almost 12 years of her life as a man named "Keith." Once she began to connect with the Lord, though—receiving His unconditional love and following His instruction—her confusion about her sexual identity began to slowly slip away.

> I didn't know it at the time, but I was no longer being conformed to the world; I was being transformed by the renewing of my mind. A mentor would help me process what the Lord was saying, what He was walking me through, or what He was talking to me about. Both of them sat with me through some pretty rough stuff. The Lord used them as

examples of healthy women which unknowingly changed me.

As I embraced being a woman and believing it was good, believing what the Lord said about who I am, being obedient to do the things He said to do, something shifted on the inside which affected the outside. As my transformation continued and my mind was being renewed, I was becoming uncomfortable with how I was dressing. I didn't look feminine in the clothes I owned. I didn't want to wear what I had. I realized the outside was the expression of what was happening on the inside. Not only was I embracing being a woman but my femininity was beginning to leak out.

I had studied Psalm 139, which told me how I was knit together and how I was known. This time when I read through it, I saw that when the Lord said that He knit me together, He knit me together with everything I would need to be a woman and to be feminine. Even though I had lived as a man, there was a nurturing nature in me and as I embraced who I was, that nurturing nature grew. I wanted the softer things. I wanted to wear make-up. I wanted to be beautiful. To grow in this area, I purposed to make friends with women who were feminine. A dear friend who, in my opinion, is very feminine, knew of my background and took me shopping. It was the scariest, most awkward and uncomfortable thing ever. With my heart pounding, I managed to seize the moment. She took me way outside the box and after the sweating stopped, I found I liked it.[10]

The goal of truly owning our own sexual identities is not that we would become rows of lumberjacks and beauty queens. These are stereotypes of masculinity and femininity. The goal is that, as we begin to connect with our Creator, layers of masks would fall away and that—slowly but surely—we would begin to see the beautiful man or woman that God created.

Understanding our identities in Christ really, then, looks like being truly comfortable in our own skin. It looks like delighting in God's design for our sexuality as well as His design for our dreams, passions, personalities, and quirks. It looks like courageously embracing both strength and gentleness. This confidence arises from a deep and genuine knowledge that we've been created in the image of God and that we carry His beauty. In short, we "reckon ourselves": I'm not a loser, a sinner, an addict, a homosexual, or LGBTQ+. I may have *been* those things, but I'm not anymore. God says I'm a brand-new creation in Christ Jesus, and I'm a saint (see 2 Corinthians 5:17). We choose to believe it because He said it, and we thank Him for redeeming us and giving us a brand-new nature. We walk this journey closely following Jesus, the One who knows us best, and stay the course as we walk into ever-increasing freedom to be our true selves in Christ.

Questions to Ask Yourself

- Where have you been getting your sense of identity from? Think about it. Write down a list of memories that informed your beliefs about your identity and also any sayings you've heard, embarrassing moments you've had, ways you were treated, things that were said to you, ways that your body has responded to stimuli, and anything else the Lord reveals.

- Ask the Lord if there are any lies you are believing about yourself that are keeping you from embracing the reality of your new creation identity. What are they?

- Who are you now uniquely as a son or as a daughter of God? How does Jesus see you and describe you?

- What else did you learn from this chapter about your identity?

Activations

- **Set Free from Sin:** Read Romans 6:5-18 slowly a few times. What does this passage tell you about your nature (since you are a follower of Christ)? Do you believe God has set you free from sin and that you're a slave to righteousness? Read the passage over and over until you believe that you have a new nature.

- **New Creation in Christ:** Read Second Corinthians 5:17 several times and ask the Lord to show you what this means for your life—that you are a new creation. What does it mean to you personally that all the old things of your life have passed away?

- **Owning Your Identity:** Keeping in mind that you are a new creation who has been set free from sin's control, review your answers in the section of questions above.

Spend some time with the Lord and pray through any of the answers you wrote down that do not align with your new creation identity or are contrary to the teachings in the Bible. Repent for believing lies and then reject them, asking the Holy Spirit to reveal to you corresponding truths about your identity. Thank the Lord for the identity that He gave you when He created you. Write down anything the Lord reveals to you.

Notes

1. Janet Boynes, *CHANGED: #oncegay Stories,* https://changedmovement .com/stories/janet-boynes.
2. Kris Vallotton, "Are You Living in a Haunted House?" in *Spirit Wars: Winning the Invisible Battle Against Sin and the Enemy* (Michigan: Chosen Books, 2012).
3. Ibid.
4. Palmer, Wilhelm, and Koopman, "Sex Determination and Gonadal Development in Mammals," *Physiological Reviews,* Vol 87(1), Jan 2007, 1-28.
5. Michelle A. Cretella, "Gender Dysphoria in Children and Suppression of Debate," 21 *J. of Am. Physicians & Surgeons* 50, 51 (2016).
6. American Psychiatric Association, *Diagnostic and Statistical Manual of Mental Disorders,* Fifth Edition (DSM-5) (Arlington, VA: American Psychiatric Association, 2013), 829.
7. J.M. Beale and S.M. Creighton. "Long-term Health Issues Related to Disorders or Differences in Sex Development/Intersex," *Maturitas,* 2016;94:143-148. doi:10.1016/j.maturitas.2016.10.003.
8. Michelle A. Cretella, Christopher H. Rosik, A.A. Howsepian, "Sex and Gender are Distinct Variables Critical to Health: Comment on Hyde, Bigler, Joel, Tate, and van Anders" (2019), *American Psychologist*, Vol 74(7), Oct 2019, 842-844.

9. Rodger Gaskin, "I Am a New Creation," *Finding You: An Identity-Based Journey Out of Homosexuality and Into All Things New* (2020).

10. KathyGrace Duncan, "My Journey into Femininity," *Finding You: An Identity-Based Journey Out of Homosexuality and Into All Things New* (2020).

Chapter 8

ENDURING FAITH

Abraham Lincoln stands as an iconic example of an American president—eloquent, driven, a man of integrity. He led the country through the Civil War, becoming renowned for his humble wisdom. But for the thirty years before his presidency, his career was marked by a series of major setbacks. He lost his job, lost a run for state legislature, failed in business, experienced the death of his sweetheart, had a nervous breakdown, was defeated in a run for House Speaker of Illinois, was defeated in a run for Congress, lost the re-nomination, was rejected for Land Officer, was defeated in a run for Senate, was defeated for the nomination for Vice President, and was again defeated in his run for the Senate two years before becoming President of the United States.

Angela Duckworth, a psychologist at the University of Pennsylvania, has determined that this kind of perseverance, what she calls "passion and sustained persistence applied toward long-term achievement," is one of the greatest predictors of success in a person's life.[1] Lincoln had this kind of grit, so the child of illiterate parents made it to the White House. Similarly, for those of us on a journey to live out redeemed sexual identities, enduring faith is a crucial ingredient along the journey. As believers, our endurance comes from trusting that God is faithful enough to lead us into complete wholeness, even if we stumble along the way.

Could God change someone's sexual identity in an instant? Of course. He's God, so He can do whatever He wants. Bill Johnson describes it as "God's one-step program: Out of darkness and into His marvelous light!" I love stories of supernatural, instant transformation. I've had those touches from the Lord. And I encourage everyone, by all means, to be believing for God to dramatically come through for them today, even in the area of their sexuality! Romans 6 does promise us the grace to stop acting out in sexual sin the moment we surrender to Christ. However, for those of us who are walking away from believing that we are "gay," transformation may be a journey that takes some time. It's OK if temptations don't immediately flee and our unwanted sexual desires don't instantly vanish.

Although we may wish otherwise, God often seems to be more interested in doing a really deep and comprehensive work, address-ing many areas of our lives, than He is in merely transporting us to a different destination. The Bible promises that, *All things work together for good to those who love God, to those who are the called according to His purpose*" (Romans 8:28). So we know that if it's not good yet, He's not done working with us. But we have to be willing to go the distance.

To do that, we must understand the importance of faith. I remem-ber so clearly the season immediately following the miraculous phys-ical healing I received. I had discovered that God was real and that His power could change impossible situations today. So I studied and studied the concept of faith in the Bible. I read Romans 4 over and over and the various accounts of miracles performed at the hands of the apostles and the seventy disciples (see Luke 10:17). My Bible told me that *"with God all things are possible"* (Matthew 19:26), so I was determined to mine the depths of His promises.

Faith is the basic building block of our walk with God. It is the belief that God is who He says He is and does what He says He will do. Trusting in God in this way changes our lives, inviting God to move on our behalf. Even a small amount of faith, the Bible says, will move Heaven and earth (see Matthew 17:20). The wonderful thing is that we are not the source of our own faith; God is. Our *"faith comes by hearing, and hearing by the word of God"* (Romans 10:17). Our faith rests on His faithfulness. And He always finishes what He starts, even if that journey takes time (see Philippians 1:6).

For most of us, patterns of sin and broken intimacy in our lives were not created overnight. And typically, there are multiple factors in our lives that have contributed to our sexual feelings and desires. As such, it can take time to uproot and address areas of unmet need or wounding, retraining our brains with new thought patterns and reforming our key relationships. Andrew Comiskey leads a national organization called Desert Stream, and they have a ministry called Living Waters that was crucial to my journey because it addresses "the roots of sexual and relational issues that ensnare Christians into unhealthy living." Having led people through a journey of addressing sexual and relational needs for 40 years, Andrew knows firsthand that walking into lasting freedom can be a faith walk that takes time.

> My freedom from the domination of homosexuality began with a revelation of the Cross: God's radical self-giving. God gave all and all He asked is that I give Him all. That took time. Young and sexually charged, I found giving up "gay stuff" hard. I knew deep down that my ways were destructive, but I had not enough traction with Christians to

discover how divine Love could surpass my feelings. I volleyed between gay and Christian culture for a while before I "got" the Cross. Surrender to Jesus made the difference.

Second, God showed me I was created in His image—a man intended for a woman. That is an unquestionable truth but my Bible-toting world stressed what I should not do sexually rather than who I was as God's gendered guy. That invited me to dig deeper into why I was at odds with my masculinity and to get on with the business of relating to women. Gender reconciliation became a priority in my thinking and in my daily decisions. I learned how to be a good friend to guys (hard at first) and to love a woman whom I married. Best choice ever.

I also learned that unless I was rooted in a dynamic community of faith, I would be sucked back into perverting my need for love. I grew to love the real presence of Jesus in His Word and saints, in music, and in our efforts to create a home for Him. As we gathered at the first Vineyard Church in Los Angeles, He deepened authentic worship. There, my fiancé and I began to gather with gay-identified persons whom we helped to know Jesus. Together we discovered His strength perfected in weakness. That became the basis for Living Waters, a group I still run as a Catholic in my parish; our groups now flow out to every continent (desertstream.org). My well-being is bound up in helping make the broken body of Christ beautiful for Jesus.[2]

When we submit ourselves to God, we begin to shed our futile attempts at self-sufficiency—grasping at ways to fulfill our own needs—and, instead, allow the Lord to reveal His ways to us. He designed every cell in our bodies. He knows so much more than we do about how we are wired, what we need, and what true fulfillment will look like. And it takes time to trust Him, to retrain ourselves, and to learn to untangle the old patterns of thought and behavior. This is normal! As Andrew says, giving up that self-gratification is hard at times, but there is so much freedom and life on the other side of this journey. Plus, God promises that we don't have to do any of this on our own. He is with us every step of the way.

Don't Go Down There

This lesson hit home for me one day as I was walking through an airport, waiting out a layover. I was returning to Dallas after a great trip to Redding, California to visit my friends from ministry school. Coming down from the high of connecting with so many close relationships, I was walking through the airport, feeling tired and hungry. In the past, airports had been trouble spots for me. I had traveled for work, and I used to wander into the bookstores to ogle at the men depicted in the workout magazines. I would idolize their muscular bodies sprawled across the pages, simultaneously sexualizing them or wishing I could trade my body in for theirs. One model in particular had been the long-standing object of my fantasies. But that was in my past. I had gone through three life-changing years of ministry school, learning so much about my identity in Christ, and was feeling more confident than ever in who I was as a man. At this point, my addiction to porn and masturbation had incrementally faded away. I was a new person, having experienced incredible transformation.

On that day, I walked through the airport in search of food, and I saw a Subway restaurant on the lower level. *Great,* I thought, *I'll go get a sandwich.* Moving toward the escalator, I suddenly heard the Holy Spirit: "Don't go down there." Confused and a bit incredulous, I disregarded the clear warning.

That's ridiculous, I thought. I'd been doing so well in my purity journey, and it was just a sandwich. What could possibly go wrong? So, down the escalator I went. As soon as I got to the bottom, though, I looked up and found myself standing within 10 feet of the actual male model from the fitness magazines. This incredibly athletic, attractive man who had been the subject of my many fantasies was sitting directly in front of me. Wearing a tank top. In real life. I was triggered so completely that, for the first time in several victorious months replete with God-encounters, lust overwhelmed me, and I went into the bathroom, fantasized, and masturbated.

I was devastated. I'd been doing so well in my progress. I knew that wasn't who I was. That kind of behavior wasn't a part of my life anymore. But what had just happened? Incredibly discouraged, I struggled awhile to pick myself back up and realize that the Lord could use even a moment like this for my benefit.

Trigger Warning

God cares about every step of our journeys. The Holy Spirit had spoken to me, trying to protect me from my own weakness in a moment of vulnerability. And He had done so in direct response to my years of praying for His help. In that moment, when I decided to disregard His guidance, I thought I knew better than He did. I had stepped outside of my intimate relationship with Him, choosing my own will instead of trusting Him. And because of that, I exposed myself to a battle that I wasn't prepared to win.

When the Israelites left slavery in Egypt, the Bible says that *"God did not lead them by way of the land of the Philistines, although that was near; for God said, 'Lest perhaps the people change their minds when they see war, and return to Egypt.' So God led the people around by way of the wilderness of the Red Sea"* (Exodus 13:17-18). In the same way He led the Israelites, He is constantly leading us out of bondage and into His freedom. He is invested in our journey, though, and He will redirect us from a battle that we are not equipped to win. Our job is to stay close to Him and let Him guide us.

In order to remain victorious, we need to increase our self-awareness when it comes to acknowledging our mental state. There is a reason why the devil tried to tempt Jesus in the desert at the end of a 40-day fast. He looks for "opportune" times (see Luke 4:13). Our mental, emotional, and physical health are all intertwined. If we are feeling weakened in one area, it can be much easier to give in to temptation that would otherwise be resistible. Friends of mine who have experience with recovery programs like Alcoholics Anonymous have an easy way to remember the things that tend to make us especially vulnerable to temptation. It is a brilliant acronym, H.A.L.T., which stands for hungry, angry, lonely, tired.[3] My friend Mark Peterson also likes to add *bored* and *stressed*. Each of these conditions leave an individual susceptible to making decisions that he/she otherwise wouldn't choose. Looking back, I can see that, as I walked through that airport, I was definitely hungry, but I was also tired from my appointment-packed visit to Redding and feeling lonely as I left such deep, life-giving friendships behind. I hadn't been completely aware of all that was going on internally, but the Lord knew that I was in a vulnerable state. And He was warning me.

Because I was in a "H.A.L.T. condition" and had been unaware of my internal atmosphere, I stepped out of my intimate relationship with God for a moment and ignored the Holy Spirit's voice, preferring to momentarily resurrect my old dead sin nature. I had missed the mark and, whenever we do that, God invites us to quickly restore our connection with Him by turning from our sin and walking the path back into intimacy with Him. This restoration can happen within moments. We first need to get vulnerable before the Lord, confessing that what we did was sin, expressing our remorse, and asking Him to forgive us. Then, with a momentary reflection, we recall how we have surrendered our lives to Him and, from the heart, yield once again. He is Lord over our lives.

After that, we can move on to check in with our key relationships. In my airport experience, it was a significant enough misbehavior that it would be important for me to invite a trustworthy friend into my journey, confessing and sharing my experience with him and receiving his love and compassion and maybe some prayer. Finally, restoration after sin looks like reminding ourselves who and whose we are so we don't allow accusation or condemnation in. We can declare our new identities over ourselves, calling ourselves pure, clean, the spotless Bride, beloved man or woman of God, His royal priesthood.

Growth in the Process

The occasions when we trigger and act out in sin can feel like moving backwards. These moments, however, do not disqualify the beautiful, hard work of sanctification that God has already accomplished in us. They simply indicate that we have stepped back into our old identity, allowing insecurity to overwhelm our confidence in Christ. The enemy would love it if we would believe that, because we have slipped up, we have undone all of the progress we've made. He would like nothing more than to see us give up, sink into hopelessness, and believe that we have to start our journey all over at the very beginning.

But our journey into wholeness isn't a game of Chutes and Ladders. We don't suddenly slide back to the beginning. I have several friends who had some kind of a major moral fall in a season after they had experienced much breakthrough. They kept going, though, and never fell again. When we have committed to partnering with God, we are moving forward. And the Lord in His mercy uses even our triggered moments to help us grow into the fullest expression of our truest selves.

Our triggers, after all, are simply unhealed areas of pain or over-looked needs of the heart. And oftentimes the situations that spark sexual attraction actually pinpoint for us the very areas the Holy Spirit is wanting to heal. My friend Andrew Franklin shared his process with moments of same-sex attraction. He explained how he has learned to recognize his triggers for what they are. Instead of experiencing same-sex attraction and giving those feelings the authority over his life, he checks in with his heart and with God. "When I experience [a moment of same-sex attraction], I know I can go back to God and ask, 'What's going on? Did something happen to make me insecure or anxious?' Because, I've learned that that is where same-sex attraction comes from for me."[4]

When we have unmet emotional needs, it is possible for them to become sexualized. As we saw in Chapter 2, sex is deeply intimate. But acting out sexually will not bring the fulfillment we crave. What our hearts want is to be seen, to be known, to be comforted, to be accepted, to be safe. God is there to help us grow in understanding our own triggers so that He can heal the pain and meet the actual needs of our hearts. When we get triggered or become sexually aroused in an undesired situation, we can stop and ask the Lord—without shame—*why* we're experiencing this attraction. We can then listen to hear His counsel. These moments are actually invitations for resolution and for greater intimacy with God—if we will just lean in and stay the course.

Never, Never, Never Give Up

Cecil Jackman endured repeated abuse within his home and outside of it. His journey highlights the difference between grit and enduring faith. Grit is a wonderful attribute and an important character trait, but it finds its limits within the human will. Faith, however, leans upon the strength and faithfulness of God. Enduring faith means that we are not only determined to walk this path to wholeness, but we are also acknowledging that the all-powerful One is walking alongside us, empowering us with His grace and covering us with His mercy.

> I was raised in church through the end of middle school. Growing up, I bonded with girls more than boys. My grandma was also my biggest love. I didn't bond with my dad. He was a workaholic and abusive both verbally and physically.
>
> I was sexually abused from a young age, raped at age four by my babysitter in the bathtub. I felt that if I had been a girl, she wouldn't have done that to me. At school, my third-grade teacher's aide told the entire class I was a homosexual

and explained in detail what that meant. My nickname became Cecil the Homo through the eighth grade. In eighth grade, I was fondled by my male teacher. Not being good at sports involving a ball, I was constantly made fun of in gym class, which further ostracized me from boys my age.

In college, I became a frequent at the adult bookstore. I became addicted to hardcore gay porn and masturbation, though I had no relations until I was 26.

I decided I would be a good, celibate, gay Christian man. I decided to work as hard as I could for God so He'd free me. But change never happened. So after a couple of years of serving in every ministry I could find, I became convinced God hated me.

At 26, I ran into a gay cousin I hadn't seen in years. The next night, we went to a gay bar. I felt free. I was with guys like me. But while I sat there having a beer, I felt like God said, "What are you doing here?" So I stood up, told my cousin I had to go home, and left. The next week, I felt that same conviction to leave, but this time I drank my beer, partied, and had sex with another man.

I had only technically come out for two months, but I hit bottom fast. One night when I was driving home from a night of gay clubbing, I realized I wasn't feeling the sense of connection to God anymore. It left me feeling alone and empty. I was desperate and put myself into a rehab program in New York. The pastor there said he could help me.[5]

So, Cecil traveled up to New York, desperate for help. He joined the program and began taking steps. There was nothing easy about facing years of pain, rejection, and twisted beliefs about God. "There were times I got afraid and wanted to run. There were even some times that I quit for a few hours. I never really quit for [that long, though]. I told the Lord, 'I will commit to whatever it takes as long as I can see [what they are teaching me] in the Bible and they aren't abusing me.'" The leaders at the rehab program were kind, though, and Cecil didn't quit. Clinging to his commitment to God and the hope that there was freedom from a life of homosexual desires, he began to encounter God in a new way. Over and over again, the program pointed him to the reality of God's love for him until it finally made the journey from his head to his heart. He was loved by God and, suddenly, he understood that God was on his side and that he'd been created for a purpose.

Even with this revelation, though, the path wasn't simple or short. "I stumbled a few times, quit a few times. I messed up, but there is mercy in the journey. God's grace was powerful enough to save me when I identified as gay, and His grace and mercy were strong enough to keep me in the process of walking into wholeness. That's called the good fight of faith. It's a fight." Every time he got knocked down, he got back up and resumed the fight. One of his keys for enduring this fight of faith was worship. "In the difficult times I would get in the Word, stay in fellowship with others, and I would worship in the secret place, pouring the pain, unfairness, and fear out to God." He would share his heart honestly, but like David, he always returned to worship. And in that way, the mountains that he was facing got smaller as his view of God grew. "The change wasn't overnight, but it was continual. Seven years later, I married a woman named Christine. After the trauma and despair, I never imagined I could feel this much hope about the future."[6]

Psalm 23 says, *"Yea, though I walk through the valley of the shadow of death, I will fear no evil; for You are with me; Your rod and Your staff, they comfort me"* (Psalm 23:4). This verse points us to a few truths. There will be times when we feel like we are walking through *"the valley of the shadow of death."* I'm not sure that there's a good way to avoid that process. But fear does not need to accompany us in these valleys because His perfect love never leaves us. God is ever-present, bringing His protection and His comfort. And finally, as Kris Vallotton says, when we find ourselves walking through the valley, we must keep walking. We can't stop. This is not the place to lie down. We are to *"fight the good fight of faith,"* keeping our eyes locked on the wonder of our almighty God and the vision of wholeness given to us by His Son (1 Timothy 6:12).

Questions to Ask Yourself

- What are some disciplines you can implement into your life to help you avoid temptation and triggers that can cause you to compromise/sin?

- The next time you feel triggered or tempted sexually, what can you proactively do in that moment? Write out a few steps here that you can be ready to proactively take.

- What are some actions you could take to get yourself back on a healthy path should you find yourself repeating any familiar sinful behaviors in the future?

Activations

- **Assess Your Vulnerabilities:** Think back to a couple of times that you've compromised/sinned in the area of your purity (lust, porn, or sinful sexual activities). What was going on in your life at that time? Were you hungry, angry, lonely, tired, bored, and/or stressed? Work to become more aware of the state of your inner world when you experience the strongest temptations or moral failures. Figure out which scenarios weaken your defenses and become proactive about avoiding them or changing them promptly.

- **The Faith Chapter:** Read the faith chapter (Hebrews 11) to remind yourself of all the amazing, even impossible, breakthroughs that people who had faith in God were able to experience. Write a paragraph about why the journey you're on with your sexual identity is no more impossible than the exploits that the heroes of the faith accomplished.

Notes

1. Angela Duckworth, *Grit: The Power of Passion and Perseverance* (New York, NY: Scribner, 2016).

2. Andrew Comiskey, *CHANGED: #oncegay Stories,* https:// changedmovement.com/stories/andrew-comiskey.

3. Thaddeus Camlin, Psy.D., "Self-Care in Recovery: H.A.L.T. at the Crossroads," Practical Recovery, January 20, 2017, https://www .practicalrecovery.com/prblog/self-care-recovery-h-a-l-t-crossroads.

4. Testimony: Andrew Franklin, in discussion with CHANGED Movement staff, 2019.

5. Cecil Jackman, *CHANGED: #oncegay Stories,* https://changedmovement .com/stories//cecil-jackman.

6. Testimony: Cecil and Christine, in discussion with CHANGED Movement staff, 2019.

Chapter 9

VISION

The Lord shared His intention for each one of us when He
spoke to the prophet Jeremiah: *"'I know the plans I have for you,' declares
the Lord, 'plans to prosper you and not to harm you, plans to give you
hope and a future'"* (Jeremiah 29:11 NIV). Without understanding our
new identities in Christ, without grasping the astonishing reality that
we are no longer sinners but saints, it is very difficult to envision the
hope-filled future that God wants to give us. But this final key in our
journey is a crucial one. Proverbs says that, *"Where there is no vision,
the people perish"* (Proverbs 29:18 KJV). During the Revolutionary War,
George Washington flew an unofficial flag of the United States over his
soldiers as they fought in extremely brutal conditions. This flag had no
international significance yet; it had no monetary value in and of itself.
But thousands of men laid down their lives for the vision of a free
America that was symbolized by that piece of cloth.[1]

Having a vision for our futures helps us to overcome present hur-
dles, refines our focus, and keeps our perspective on the bigger picture.
The Bible says that Jesus endured the unimaginable sorrow, physical
torture, and absolute rejection of the cross *"for the joy that was set
before Him"* (Hebrews 12:2). With a vision of His purpose, knowing that
His sorrow and suffering would not last forever, Jesus allowed Himself
to be crucified. His vision of the future joy cast a bigger shadow than

His present pain. That is powerful vision! Those of us who are leaving behind a homosexual life need to follow His lead. Casting a vision of complete freedom and wholeness for our lives can be a challenge when all we can see is present sin and temptation and past pain, but the Lord invites us to dream with Him about our future. He encourages us to think, "OK, if I'm a new creation, then what does my future look like?"

God is invested in our lives, and He has things He wants to say to us about our futures. So, we can start by trusting that His vision for our lives is good. And we can ask Him to reveal that to us. In my case, the vision for my life was marriage and children. That may not be the vision for every person who has struggled with homosexuality, though. God may give people visions for business, ministries, books to be written, music to be performed, cities to be impacted. Every person is unique, and the Lord knows what He designed each one of us to accomplish and what will make us come alive.

In Habakkuk, the prophet poses some challenging questions to the Lord. He is living through difficult times, imploring God to bring judgment on Judah's wickedness. Habakkuk has a timeline of breakthrough, though, that the Lord is apparently not meeting. Instead of being frustrated with His prophet's doubt, God assures him that He's on top of it. *"I will work a work in your days which you would not believe, though it were told you"* (Habakkuk 1:5). As the prophet aligns himself with God's word, the Lord encourages him to *"Write the vision and make it plain on tablets, that he may run who reads it. …Though it tarries, wait for it; because it will surely come"* (Habakkuk 2:2-3). There are times when our ability to enter into future breakthrough requires us to write out the vision that we have been given by God and "make it plain" so that we can continue to run our race, trusting that God will lead the way.

Vision for Family

Early on in my journey, I took this idea literally. On six sheets of paper, I wrote out Second Corinthians 5:17: *"Therefore, if anyone is in Christ, he is a new creation; old things have passed away; behold, all things have become new."* I then placed them in my bathroom, above my bed, in the living room, and in the kitchen. A friend came over once and, confused, he thought I was trying to send him a message. But I said, "Oh, no! Those aren't for you. They're for me!" At that stage in my journey, I needed to place the truth of my new identity in front of my face at all times. I needed a constant reminder—a vision—of the promised reality that was warring to manifest fully within me.

Because at that point, I was still feeling aroused by other men. In those confusing moments, my body's physical reaction felt like a greater truth than my new identity in Christ. It felt like I wasn't making any progress. But that is a carnal perspective. My friends Steve and Wendy Backlund, who have incredible insight on the power of believing and appropriating God's Word in our lives, like to say, "Any area of our lives that is not glistening with hope is under the influence of a lie." When we use our circumstances, rather than God's Word as they suggest, to define our reality, we are limiting ourselves to an earthly experience. But our life in Christ is different. As born-again believers, we walk in the Spirit. Our conclusions about life are drawn from the Holy Spirit and from God's Word, not from the temporal conditions of our present realities.

Early in my journey, I was constantly battling between my physical and emotional experience and the reality of who God said I was. I needed the truth of Second Corinthians to surround me, to remind me that I was a new creation and that all things were possible for me. I didn't have to look at my future based upon where I had been.

Bluntly stated, my sexual arousals didn't have the power to erase my "all things have become new" new-creation identity. My future was in the hands of the Creator of the Universe.

Hearing God's vision for my life from other people also helped me to sustain the journey. The gift of prophecy, when used correctly, can bring incredible encouragement to our lives. Jill Stacher was a powerful female leader in my church who was known for praying two hours a day and prophesying accurately. She said to me once, "Your wife is coming, and she's going to be fire!" At that point in my journey, I honestly couldn't imagine being sexually aroused by a female, much less being married and having a family, but those were deep desires of my heart. That prophetic word gave me a vision for my future, building my faith that this battle wouldn't last forever. I was making progress.

I had told the Lord that I wasn't going to fake it. I had never really been sexually attracted to women, so I'd decided that, if that never changed, I wouldn't get married. I wasn't even going to date a woman if I didn't feel attracted to her. Every woman deserves to be with someone who adores her, and I didn't want to bring pain to someone's life like that. But the Lord invited me to have the vision of being married to a woman to whom I felt sexually attracted. So, from time to time along my journey, I would remind myself of that God-inspired vision or prophetic promise from God to me, especially in seasons further along in my journey.

Red-Haired Bombshell

I had dated a few girls in high school, college, and the years following. I was blessed to spend time with some ladies who were beautiful on the inside and out. But to my disappointment, any feelings I'd had for them were fledgling, inconsistent, felt like pressure to maintain, and were very quickly dismissed as an anomaly; the same-sex attraction was always immensely stronger. Until one day. The girl with the long hair and the sparkly belt was sitting across the room from me. Her name was Tiffany.

Tiffany was the first woman whom I found myself captivated by. I couldn't believe it, but I felt unable to take my eyes off of this girl! And after I got to know her, I wanted to be around her all of the time. I admired her more than anyone. She was so pure and kind, so loving and beautiful, the best listener in the world, and incredibly thoughtful. And, praise the Lord, I discovered that I was physically attracted to her. I thought she was stunning. Beautiful! But it was deeper than that. I was totally taken by *who* she was. Our conversations were magical. I had never been capable of that experience or those feelings before. This was evidence that God must have been at work renewing my mind. As I pondered how God had brought me to this place, Jill Stacher's words came to my mind. This red-haired girl must be the lady who would "be fire!"

Eventually, as we started dating, I realized that I was going to need to tell Tiffany about my past struggles. I was going to have to tell this gorgeous, innocent young woman that I had been addicted to masturbation, gay pornography, and that I'd had some homosexual interactions. If we were considering sharing our lives together, I knew that she deserved to know everything. But I had no idea how she would respond.

On a road trip to visit some friends, I felt the desire to share my story with Tiffany bubble up in my heart. Our plan was, after seeing our friends, to head on to her family's house for Thanksgiving and stay through the weekend. We had been dating for about six weeks, and it definitely felt as if the relationship was headed toward a future together. We were driving along and, just as I had the thought that this was my time to share with her, a song came on the Christian radio station.

"Oh, I love this artist," Tiffany said.

"I do, too!" I responded.

"Yeah, she's the best. Isn't it sad about what happened to her?" Confused, I wasn't sure what she was talking about. She explained to me that the artist had recently come out as gay. "I just have a heart for her," Tiffany said. "I hope she's OK." Immediately, I felt such gratitude that the Lord would've given me a girlfriend who had such compassion for people who were struggling with same-sex attraction. Literally one second after I'd felt prodded by the Holy Spirit to share my testimony with her, God had orchestrated this interaction so I could see her gentle, understanding heart. Emboldened by this event, I began to share my story.

"Well, actually, I have some history with that." I told her about my struggles, my sexual history, and the journey of restoration that the Lord had brought me on during the last several years. Because of His grace and the work that He had done in my life, I explained to her, I was now hardly experiencing any same-sex attraction. Instead, I was attracted to her, which was new for me. She listened empathetically, assuring me that she understood, that she accepted me, and that this wasn't going to be a problem for our dating relationship.

I was over the moon. I had just shared the scariest part of my testimony and my girlfriend had totally understood! How incredible! And what a relief!

She asked if we could pull over for a pit stop, so I stopped and got gas, my heart feeling light with relief and joy. What I wouldn't know until months later was that, at that same time, Tiffany was in the truck stop bathroom experiencing an absolute panic attack. Having held it together during my story, responding with such grace and compassion to me, she'd made it to the restroom before completely melting down. Fearful thoughts raced through her head: *I have feelings for this guy! It's been going so well, and then he tells me that he has this homosexual past?! We're supposed to be going to my family's place for Thanksgiving! What do I do now?*

Totally freaked out and confused, she heard the Lord's voice interrupt her anxious thoughts: "Don't you ever look at him that way again; because I don't." Suddenly sobered, she realized that the Lord had a vision for my life, and she needed to get on board with His view of me. In His eyes, my past was behind me—dead and gone—and so she had no right to view me that way anymore. Leaning on that word from the Lord, she left the bathroom and joined me for the rest of our trip.

Hearing those words from God didn't mean that the conversation was over. The Lord wasn't asking Tiffany to avoid her feelings or ignore the questions that arose as she processed this new information. The Lord had given her a vision for my life, but she also needed to know where I currently was on my journey of walking out my freedom. We had multiple conversations in the following days about my past. She needed to process all that I'd told her with me, she needed the freedom to ask me questions, and she needed more information so that she could understand me better. I welcomed these conversations, and I encouraged her to talk to my friends and mentors who had seen me walk out this journey. As I became more and more secure in my identity in Christ, shame had no hold on me. I knew the freedom that the Lord had brought to my life, and I wanted Tiffany to feel safe and to share that sense of confidence.

We dated for a few more months, were engaged for six months after that, and now have been married for almost 15 years. When Tiffany shared the full picture of her coming to grips with my past, including the truck stop breakdown, it didn't hurt me to hear of her confusion. I had compassion for her fear, but what amazed me was how God spoke to her. "Don't you ever look at him that way again; because I don't." It was yet another confirmation of my identity. God didn't see me as gay. He only saw me as His redeemed son. It gave me increased vision for my future.

When we come to Christ, He makes us new creations. God's vision for our lives is not restricted by our weaknesses, our temptations, or our failures. As we grow in our intimacy with Him, we get to step into *the reality* that we are a new creation. We get to experience our true identities, living fully from that place as a son or a daughter. We are seated in heavenly places with Christ, no longer merely human, but Spirit-led beings for whom all things are possible. Keeping God's vision before us as we walk toward wholeness will anchor us in His promises. And, as my friend Angel Colon experienced, it just might save our lives.

Pulse Redemption

Angel and his good friend Luis Javier Ruiz organized the Freedom March in Orlando. They had been sharing publicly about the transformation God had brought to their hearts and their sexuality. It was incredibly powerful to hear their stories, as they had both been present in the early hours of June 12, 2016, when a man opened fire at Pulse, a gay nightclub in Orlando, killing 49 people and injuring 53 more. In the midst of that horrific night, Angel encountered God.

My life before I pursued change in my sexuality was what I would call "a hot mess." Lonely, empty, unhappy, shackled, and unloved were the ways I felt for eight years after I came out. The more unhappy I was, the worse it got. My life was so consumed by homosexuality, drugs and liquor that I wouldn't give the time of day to my family. Having been raised in a strong Christian home, I felt a deep conflict between what I had known to be good and right and the life I was living.

I woke up hungover on June 11th, 2016, after a night of drinking and drug use. That evening my friends and I went to Pulse, a club in Orlando. At 2:02 a.m., everything changed. While saying our goodbyes, we heard a big POP! I dropped my drink, realizing the sounds were gunshots. As we ran, I was shot several times and fell down, pulling my friends with me. Struggling to stand back up, I felt a foot step behind my left leg and heard a loud snap which resulted in my left femur breaking. I couldn't move or even feel my legs, so I covered my head and stayed still. What followed was chaos all around me. I started comforting the lady lying next to me, whispering to her to pretend to be dead.[2]

Bleeding from his wounds, with a broken leg, Angel was trapped as he heard the shooter moving intentionally around the room, one by one shooting everyone on the floor who was still alive. The woman next to him began to scream hysterically as the shooter walked closer and closer to where they lay. "I told her, 'You need to be quiet. He's coming over here. You need to be quiet. Pretend you're dead!'" But as the shots came closer and closer, the woman screamed louder.

Terrified, Angel tried to slow his own breathing, close his eyes and pretend that he was already dead. As he did that, he heard a loud pop behind him. He opened his eyes. The woman whose hand he had been holding was dead. He panicked and prepared himself for the end.

"I said to myself, 'Angel, calm down. You're about to die. You're about to die.' I could feel this evil presence behind me...where you know someone is just staring at you." He could feel the shooter standing over him as he lay completely exposed in the middle of the dance floor, but no shots came. He said to himself, "All right, Angel, this is the moment the Lord has given you to make peace with Him, because you're about to die now." He started to pray, repenting and asking God for forgiveness, confessing his love, and pleading with God to take him to be with Him because he was about to die. Still, nothing was happening. The shooter was just standing behind him.

But suddenly something shifted, and Angel became aware of the spiritual warfare happening over him. "I could feel the evil and the good on top of me, fighting for my life." As soon as that happened, his prayers changed. "I changed my prayer, and I started prophesying to the Lord. I said, 'Lord, I'm not leaving here dead today. You promised my mom that her son had a purpose in life... I'm leaving here alive. And, when I leave here alive, I'm going to worship You for the rest of my life.'" As soon as he began to make these declarations over his own life, the atmosphere began to change as he experienced the authority he had in Christ.

"At the moment that I said, 'Amen,' I heard a loud pop! I felt my body jump up and down; I felt heat in my midsection, and I saw black." Angel thought he was dead. But then he came to and heard the shooter's footsteps walking away, into another room of the club. He suddenly saw the light of a police officer's flashlight coming through the door. "I raised my hands, calling out: 'Please come get me! I'm alive!'" With

shots still ringing out through the club, the officer dra[g]
over bodies and broken glass. His femur was broken, he'[d]
six times, he'd have to relearn how to walk, but he was saved.

He Will Achieve Infinitely More

Angel's journey of transformation began in those early morning hours as he lay bleeding on the floor of the nightclub. His spirit rose up in him, grasping on to the vision for his life that the Lord had given to his mom when he was still in her womb. And he used that revelation to battle the demonic forces that night. His journey hasn't been simple or quick, but Angel received a vision of how God saw him—made in His image and filled with His purpose—and that became a driving force for his transformation. This kind of change is at the very heart of the Gospel. God is present with us, and He is deeply, intimately invested in our lives. There may be many voices in the world telling us that leaving behind homosexuality is not possible, but the Creator of the Universe, the One who breathed life into our lungs, has said that it is. He has promised that, if we lay our lives in His hands, He will do more than we could ever imagine was possible. Our job is to let His vision for us take root in our lives, trusting that, as we delight ourselves in Him, we will experience the desires of our hearts (see Psalm 37:4).

As we conclude these six keys of transformation, I want to pray Paul's prayer for the Ephesian believers over you. These words come from the heart of God, delivered through a man who had experienced one of the most radical repentance stories in the Bible. From hunting Christians down in cold blood to becoming radically devoted to the Body of Christ, Paul is a living example of the transformative power of

…ired words sink deep into your heart
…ls you:

…re the Father of our Lord Jesus,
…er of every father and child in
…' I pray that he would unveil
…ies of his glory and favor until
…, strength floods your innermost being with his
divine might and explosive power.

Then, by constantly using your faith, the life of Christ will be released deep inside you, and the resting place of his love will become the very source and root of your life.

Then you will be empowered to discover what every holy one experiences—the great magnitude of the astonishing love of Christ in all its dimensions. How deeply intimate and far-reaching is his love! How enduring and inclusive it is! Endless love beyond measurement that transcends our understanding—this extravagant love pours into you until you are filled to overflowing with the fullness of God!

Never doubt God's mighty power to work in you and accomplish all this. He will achieve infinitely more than your greatest request, your most unbelievable dream, and exceed your wildest imagination! He will outdo them all, for his miraculous power constantly energizes you.

Now we offer up to God all the glorious praise that rises from every church in every generation through Jesus Christ—and all that will yet be manifest through time and eternity. Amen!
(Ephesians 3:14-21 TPT)

Questions to Ask Yourself

- As you've read this book, has the Lord revealed to you any information about your future or the vision that He wants you to have for your life going forward? What has He shown you?

- Have you received any prophetic words that felt divinely inspired that relate to your future? Write them down.

- Are there any Bible verses that feel personal and most relevant to your individual life? Which ones?

Activations

- **Seek God for Vision:** Spend some uninterrupted time with the Lord in worship and prayer. Ask Him to reveal to you more about His desires for your future. Write anything down that comes to mind. Take this information as well as the answers you wrote in the question section above and pray over them. Ask God to show you which parts of that information are most important and how you can cooperate with His vision for you. Write down the ideas that come to mind. Write up the information into a clear, simplified format—a vision statement for your life. And also include key scriptures, prophetic words, and revelations. Then, show these to a few trusted spiritual advisors in your life. Ask for their input and for what they feel is God's vision for your future.

- **Declarations:** After completing the above activation, add to your vision statement paper any other relevant input from your spiritual advisors. Make a few copies of this and post them in places where you can be reminded frequently (your car, your bathroom, your kitchen, etc.). Several times per week, pray into your vision and ask for God's grace, guidance, and favor. Declare boldly that you will do the things within your God-given vision. And thank God for His leadership in your life.

Notes

1. "American Revolution Flags," Revolutionary War and Beyond, May 1, 2020, https://www.revolutionary-war-and-beyond.com/american -revolution-flags.html.

2. Angel Colon, *CHANGED: #oncegay Stories,* https://changedmovement .com/stories/angel-colon.

3. *Homosexuality and the Church: BSSM Advanced Ministry Training 2019-2020 Year,* "Session 7: Wholehearted Surrender with Luis Javier Ruiz and Angel Colon, Orlando Pulse Nightclub Shooting Survivors," Equipped to Love.

Chapter 10

THE FRUIT OF THE BATTLE

On the evening of August 12, 2006, the delicate song "Dawn" by Jean-Yves Thibaudet began to play and the largest wedding party ever seen at my childhood church of 25,000 members proceeded to walk down the aisle. I was getting married to the woman who surpassed even my wildest dreams. Flanked by 12 groomsmen and 12 bridesmaids, I felt the weight and honor of the moment. My focus during the past years hadn't been on making it to the altar with a woman at my side. My focus had been on walking with God. Yet His goodness had led me to this point. I'd walked a long road of growth and healing to find myself standing here. And I was now the man who got the privilege of holding this gorgeous woman's hands while we pledged our lives to one another. There was no doubt in my mind that marrying Tiffany was exactly what I wanted to do, and that confidence, in itself, felt miraculous. Our wedding was an epic event! And I loved every minute of it.

We began the ceremony by worshiping together with our 400 guests, filling the church chapel with praise. My dad stood by my side as my best man. My growth process had solidified our connection, and I couldn't imagine not giving him that place of honor. There had been many, many moments on my personal journey when I felt sure I would never fall in love with a woman and get married. But at that moment, our community stood with us, backing our union, saying "yes" to the man that I had become and saying "yes" to the belief that I should be entrusted with the life of this beautiful girl. It felt like the decade or more of hard work, leaning into my relationship with God, had led to this moment. God's presence and affirmation were palpable. I raised my hands in amazement as we worshiped.

After the ceremony, we were ready to celebrate! Deliriously happy, the reception flew by in a blur for us and, in what felt like five minutes, we were on our way to the honeymoon suite. One of my guy friends, Casey, had driven over an hour to decorate the hotel room for the wedding night. So, when we arrived, we were greeted with a gorgeous penthouse suite filled with tea lights, music playing in the background, and fruit and champagne waiting to be consumed. It was absolutely beautiful.

The whole wedding had felt precious to me, showing me the indescribable goodness of my God. I—not some other man—was able to freely stand, in love, before my friends and family committing the rest of my life to my beautiful bride. I was the man who shook everyone's hand at the reception. And now, I was the man who had orchestrated this beautiful honeymoon suite for my bride. I was so proud to be able to give that moment to her. I carried her across the threshold, both of us delighted. We went out onto the balcony, sitting together, and I pulled out my list of "100 things I love about you." I read them out loud to her. It was my way of setting the tone of our wedding night—I wanted everything that happened that night to be built on honor and on our emotional and spiritual connection.

Feeling so in love and happy, we moved to the bedroom, where everything was going wonderfully. That is, until I realized that although I was, shall we say, "into it," I couldn't arrive at orgasm. I knew that wasn't normal. "Guys are normally supposed to be too quick to finish,"

I thought. *What is wrong with me?* And suddenly, every lie that I'd wrestled with for the past decades, everything I thought I had put to rest as I stood beside my bride in front of our friends and family, rose up like a wall of terror before me.

I began to panic. Thoughts began to race through my mind, painful and filled with dread: *See, all that freedom I felt at the wedding was an illusion. I'm much more damaged than I thought. I'll never be enough for her.* Flooded with anxiety and feeling suddenly completely alone, I tried to figure out what was wrong with me. I was attracted to my wife. Even before the wedding, I was regularly aware of my physical attraction to her. So then, why was my body not cooperating? And who in the world can you tell this to? You're not supposed to have to call for help on your wedding night. Right?

Tempted to be utterly humiliated, and terrified that my transformation hadn't been as complete as I thought it had been, I turned to the one person whom I felt the closest with to let her in on my tragic failure as a man: "Tiffany, I don't know what's wrong. I feel so ashamed. I feel like a failure."

She turned to me, surprised at the depth of my emotion, and said tenderly and easily, "It's no big deal. We'll figure this out. Don't worry about it. You're OK. I love you!" In that moment, she communicated something profound to my heart. She had married me for me—all of me—the good, the bad, and the ugly. She loved me, the whole person. The masculinity that I was able to offer was enough for her.

The fact that I didn't have an orgasm our first night together had triggered my wildest fears about my past, my journey, and my ability to be a husband. The enemy had tried to minimize my identity, once again, by defining *me* as my sexual *behavior*. The love of God and my new wife, though, dismantled that limited perspective. I suddenly realized that Tiffany genuinely loved me unconditionally. This was a big deal to me, yet it wasn't to her. And that love called me out of my fear and back into my true identity. Instead of allowing me to fixate on my fears and seeming inadequacy, she invited me—her husband—to lean back into the thing that had carried me to where we were—our intimacy and rich love for each other.

With that one interaction, the storm inside of me calmed. I had been nearly consumed by my fear in that moment of doubt. The enemy had tried to isolate me, whispering to my heart that this was merely evidence for what he'd been trying to tell me all along: I hadn't really changed, I would never be man enough, and I would be a disappointment to my beautiful bride. The battle over my mind had flared up— white-hot—inside of me. But the cool balm of authentic love, God's truth, and the connection that Tiffany and I had cultivated smothered the fire. Fear had threatened to rob us, but true intimacy had won out. The focus on intimacy that had led me *to* the honeymoon night, I realized, had also led me *through* the honeymoon night.

Incredibly relieved at Tiffany's grace and reoriented by her assurance, I relaxed. I realized that I didn't need to tackle a new problem in my life, inspect myself for hidden sin, read a sex book, or even repent. I remembered that God was the one who led me on this whole journey, and He was right there with me. I needed to get my focus back onto my bride, the one I loved. This wasn't supposed to be about me. Lovemaking should be about giving all our love away to this one special person. I needed to focus on her. And I needed to give back the precious, unconditional love that had been offered to me, first by God and then by my young wife. In the face of isolating, condemning fear, Tiffany had revealed God's heart for me: "I love you, and I'm with you." Unconditional love had scattered the enemy's lies. The next morning, our sexual intimacy expressed the relational and spiritual intimacy that had been solidified the night before. And it was never a problem again.

Entering the Promised Land

When the Israelites first approached the promised land, they sent in 12 spies to check things out. When those 12 men came back, they were carrying evidence of the fruitfulness of that land with them. But they were also carrying their old mindsets of self-sufficiency, lack, and fear. Ten of those men declared that the land was too dangerous, the giants that inhabited the area were too big, and the Israelites were too weak after their flight from Egypt. Only Joshua's and Caleb's minds had transformed enough, by that point, to argue that the giants—no matter how big—didn't stand a chance against the promises of God. But as the saying goes, it only took God one day to get the Israelites out of slavery in Egypt, but it took 40 years to get Egypt out of the Israelites. Those 40 years were a process in which God continually invited His people to lay down the mindsets that 400 years of slavery had instilled in them. He wanted them to learn to trust Him above everything else.

When the Israelites finally entered their promised land, 40 years later, they still had those giants to fight. But their mindsets were different. They had a history of God's faithfulness to bring to mind. They now understood that, if God was inviting them into a battle, He would make the way for victory. And they chose to cross over the Jordan River into their promised land after their 40-year journey of transformation. Like the Israelites, when I was hit by that fear on my honeymoon night, there was an opportunity for me to turn around and return to an inferior but familiar mindset. I could have fallen back into old patterns of thought from which I had spent years untangling myself. Fear always speaks to you with familiar lies about yourself, disguising itself as rational thought and making faith look illogical.

Instead, the depth of my relationship with God and the gentle love of my wife acted like a lighthouse, calling me back to the place where I could say, "No. I remember. God is an ever-present help. He's always there." In that moment, I stepped even more fully into my new-creation reality. By turning from the fear and reconnecting with God instead of my temporal circumstances, I got to experience the supernatural realm even in my sexuality. With the support of my wife, I was able to step out into the Jordan River with the Israelites, watch as the waters parted before me, and cross into my promised land. Because, once we truly get to know God, trusting in His goodness, faithfulness, and mercy is the only truly logical choice.

Those 40 years of touring the desert included some pretty serious bumps along the way. And our transformation journey is no different. There are giants of past thinking, old mentalities, and unprocessed pain standing in our promised land that we need to overcome. But as you can hear in my friend David Reece's story, God is forever faithful. He has equipped us for every battle we face, and He will not leave our side as we learn to inhabit the freedom that He has promised.

> From the time I was age three to seventeen, my life was marked by addiction to pornography, same-sex porn, unhealthy relationships, confused identity and sexual abuse. I lived a duplicitous life with a lot of behind-closed-doors behavior. I seemed like a great kid. No one suspected I was in pain, but I was lonely and confused.
>
> My cousin molested me from age three to sixteen. From the age of four, I was attracted to other boys. In high

school, I was addicted to porn and had encounters with other boys, so I thought maybe I was gay. But when a close friend came out, I knew it wasn't what I wanted and made a conscious decision not to go down that path.

In college, I didn't act out in homosexual behavior but used pornography to comfort myself in my loneliness and feelings of insufficiency. When I met my wife in 2008, she was the first person I was honest with about my lifelong addiction to porn and same-sex attraction. I was very attracted to her, but I didn't know how to reconcile that with the conflict raging within me.

In 2010 we married, and I took my porn addiction into our marriage. By the second year of marriage things got really rough. I knew I desperately needed help. One night a friend told me about a program he was in that was helping him experience [breakthrough] and understand his sexuality, and he encouraged me to check it out. That was the turning point for me. Right away I started counseling sessions that helped me get out of pain and confusion and understand that just because I was molested at three didn't mean I was gay. Then I went through a 21-week program directed at sexual issues and relational trauma. In 2015, through counseling and the 21-week program, I experienced freedom and healing from the trauma that had been causing all my pain and sexual confusion, and it's been an acceleration ever since.

Before I walked out of same-sex attraction, I only knew fake happiness. Today my life is crazy good and full of joy. For the first time in my life, I have freedom and clarity, and things keep getting clearer every day. I'm finally genuinely connected to myself and others, I have confidence in relationships and in myself, and everything is so much clearer now.[1]

A Worthy Battle

This battle for wholeness is worth it. And not only for the sexual identity transformation. Even those of us who are just at the beginning of that journey or, for whatever reason, are not experiencing relief from same-sex desires can trust that there is an infrastructure of intimacy being built inside of us that will benefit every aspect of our lives. Experiencing freedom from a struggle with same-sex attraction has changed my life, but other qualities have also been built within me simply by engaging with this battle. So, take heart. Even if you cannot see it yet, when we submit to God's plans for our lives, He takes every weak thing and builds something beautiful. It's not just the freedom from torment, confusion, and pain, though. While those are powerful and wonderful incentives to begin the journey, I can look back at my life and see that engaging in this battle for my sexual identity has shaped attributes within my personality and character that otherwise I would not have.

By nature, I see things in black and white more than shades of gray. And in my youth, I was intolerant, prideful, and prone to fear and outbursts of anger. My battle with same-sex attraction grabbed my attention early in life and sent me down a focused discipleship process that addressed my sexuality as well as many character issues. Today, I find that I am usually able to offer compassion to others easily because of all that was given to me. I was an absolute mess for a long time, but I experienced the welcoming grace of other people throughout my journey. And it is my privilege now to extend that grace to others. I see this play out with my kids, as well. There were so many times throughout my life when I missed the mark, when I fell back into sin or made the wrong choice. Again and again, I received God's grace. Because of my experience, I can bring that grace into my parenting—setting a standard for attitude and behavior, but giving grace when my kids miss the mark.

Any version of pride starts to feel a bit phony when you've had to show God and others the true mess of your inner world. But what starts with a feeling of humiliation turns into a true humility. I know who I am—a son of God—but I have no doubt in my mind that everything good in me is entirely by God's grace. I am here, living a healthy, happy life because of Him. And I am completely dependent on Him every day. I know I'm not always right—a realization my wife probably feels particularly grateful for—because I've seen how truly wrong I can be.

There are many ways that my personality has been shaped by the struggle I had with homosexuality, but part of what the Lord has done is to wipe out the fear of man from my life. In many ways, during the first part of my life, I overdosed on fear and people-pleasing. As I've talked about before, I was obsessed with what authority figures and, in particular, certain guys thought about me to the point that I didn't actually know my own mind. But at some point, I had to let that go. As I got to know who God truly was, the fear of the Lord became much more relevant to my life than the fear of man. So the kid who wore a disguise into the Christian bookstore now is the man who tells his story in front of large crowds of people. The guy who was terrified to even walk past a men's locker room now teaches whole groups of men about healthy masculinity. Now, try and tell me that God doesn't have a sense of humor!

Each year of this journey with God, I have become more and more comfortable in my own skin. I experience the wonderful feeling of living free of a guilty conscience because I no longer engage in sexual sin, sexual fantasy, porn, or masturbation. The greatest gift that this battle has brought to my life, though, is increased intimacy. I have a wonderful marriage, I have great sex with my wife, I no longer get sexually aroused by men, I have deep friendships, and I am emotionally available to mentor a whole new generation of individuals who are discovering God's invitation into new levels of freedom. I tell my kids that I love them every day. And I constantly am working to show them affection. None of this would have been possible for me before this journey. I wasn't even able to hug anyone until my late twenties. Touch was too complicated, too personal for me. Intimate relationships with others seemed light years away from the isolation that I occupied. But God knew that I was made for connection, and He knew how to get me here.

So many people who are in the midst of struggling with homosexuality cannot even imagine living a life of connection, let alone deep intimacy with others. It only makes sense, though, that our very place of weakness would be the place that God's redemption would shine the brightest. That's just how He works. Jeff Johnston's life displays this transformation clearly.

> At five years old, I engaged in sexual play and was introduced to sexual things by other young boys in my neighborhood. That caused me to pull back from connecting with other boys because I didn't want that to happen again. So, I tended to connect more with girls. In junior high, I discovered pornography and got hooked on it. I felt shame and guilt, afraid that someone would find out what

I was doing. I became even more disturbed when my fascination with pornography began to shift from women to men. But I worked to maintain an outer image of being fine for years, even as the sexual addiction and homosexual attraction increased.

Then in my early 20s I went to Australia as a missionary for several years. When I came back, I was working with a high school group and was reaching the end of my rope. The contrast between struggling intensely with my sexuality and being involved in the church was extremely difficult.

But during that time, I went to a conference.... It was the first time I had heard anyone talk about potential reasons behind same-sex attraction or that it was possible to leave homosexuality. That conference was a turning point for me, and within a week I started going to a support group for people who also wanted to leave homosexuality. I had kept this part of my life hidden for years, but slowly I began talking to friends and family about my struggle. Where I feared rejection, I usually found compassion and concern. I also started seeing a Christian counselor, attended conferences about healing sexuality, and found some books on the issue. These were all very instrumental in bringing about change and [wholeness] in my life.

Although I started out strong in my journey out of homosexuality, I went through a period of time where I really questioned my faith and my identity as a Christian. I started going to clubs and having sex with men I had just met. There was a lot of talk about HIV/AIDS during that time, and I knew my choices were very unsafe.

Finally, I made a return to my faith and to the church. Instead of pursuing a role in leadership, I just focused on pursuing healthy, non-sexual relationships with men. I had a mentor, and I got involved in weekly accountability relationship groups. I had guy friends who loved and accepted me where I was but who would also call me out when I did things that weren't good for me. And I realized that my struggle wasn't that different from some of their struggles. Those relationships were incredibly healing and transformative for me.

A few years later, I began leading a group at my church, and a young lady came, who I thought was cute. Judy and I ended up dating, then getting married. We are still married and have a healthy relationship and have three sons together. Our oldest is 20, and we have twins who are 17.[2]

Memorial Stones

The greatest gift that has come out of this battle, beyond my wonderful wife and four beautiful kids, has been my relationship with God. I no longer feel that I have to hide from the Lord like Adam, covering himself with fig leaves. Shame is gone. I get to walk with my Father in the cool of the day. I have experienced the ultimate freedom by living aligned with His design for my life. Of course, we don't need to battle homosexuality to know the Lord intimately, but there is something remarkable about this journey. Those of us who have walked this road end up knowing Him really well because there just isn't any other way through it. Life hasn't always been easy. Tiffany and I have faced some big challenges in our family's health and with our children. I have battled with deep, crippling fear. But I know who my source is. I know where to go when things get hard. I trust that God will show up for me when I need Him because we've paved that road of deep friendship together on this journey. And He does show up every time.

Once the Israelites crossed the Jordan River, Joshua instructed them to take 12 stones from the bottom of the river—one per tribe—and build a memorial of God's supernatural intervention. *"That this may be a sign among you when your children ask in the time to come, saying, 'What do these stones mean to you?' Then you shall answer them.... And these stones shall be for a memorial to the children of Israel forever"* (Joshua 4:6-7).

The places of victory, the areas of breakthrough in our lives, belong to us, to our children, and to our children's children forever. Each and every triumph in this battle builds a memorial to God's faithfulness, a touchstone of His commitment to us from which we can draw courage whenever we want. The intimacy that I built with God during this journey is one that has forever changed my life and the lives of many around me. That gift is something I get to carry with me forever. And now it is my joy to be able to give it away.

Notes

1. David Reece, *CHANGED: #oncegay Stories,* https://changedmovement .com/stories//david-reece.

2. Jeff Johnston, *CHANGED: #oncegay Stories,* https://changedmovement .com/stories/jeff-johnston.

Chapter 11

CREATING A HEALING ENVIRONMENT

Whether you have never dealt with same-sex attraction or you're just beginning to pursue wholeness and freedom in your sexual identity, you can have a hand in creating a healing environment for others. Learning how to support them in their journeys, even if we are just one step ahead of them, can have a huge impact on how freely they are able to learn or relearn intimacy. That is not to say that any one environment is perfect or that the responsibility of their growth process rests solely on the community around them. But how we react to other people's weakness, pain, and sin—especially when it's different from ours—can either hinder or encourage their journey into freedom. Learning to banish fear, release control, and speak the truth in love can create a setting in which hurting individuals can open up to real restoration.

KathyGrace Duncan, whose story I mentioned in Chapter 7, experienced two very different church environments along her journey. As a young child, she had witnessed her mother's verbal and emotional abuse at the hands of her father. Internally, she made the decision that women were weak and would get abused. It would be safer to be a boy. "As I watched him treat her the way he did, my takeaway was that women are hated, women are vulnerable, and women are weak." Subconsciously, she knew that she didn't want to be a woman because they got abused, but she also didn't want to be like her abusive father. "So, I made a vow: I'm going to be the man my dad is not."

Experiencing sexual abuse at the hands of a family member confirmed this understanding that being a woman meant being hurt by men. When KathyGrace was seven years old, her brother was born. He was so adored by everyone that something solidified in her heart. "In order to have that affirmation that I was so hungry for, I needed to be a boy." As she grew up, she became best friends with a boy who was excited that she wanted to join his biological sex. Together, they would go to school dances or the roller rink in a nearby town to dance with girls. Tired of hiding all of this from her parents, at 19 years old, she moved out of their house, began hormone treatment, and started to live as a man.

But God had a different plan. After starting to live as a man, she met a girl who kept inviting her to go to church. Finally assenting, Kathy-Grace went with her and, there, heard over and over again about Jesus. Intrigued, she answered an altar call to give her life to the Lord. But when she woke up the following morning, nothing had changed. So, she kept walking forward in response to altar calls, Sunday after Sunday, until the pastor finally told her that once was enough! Still living as a man, she didn't hear anything from the Lord about changing her lifestyle. "My interpretation of [that] was that He's OK with this. He didn't tell me it was wrong or strike me dead, so I'm moving forward with [living as a man]."

About a year later, KathyGrace's dad found out where she worked and told her boss that she wasn't a man, but she was his daughter. She got fired from her job and, because one of her co-workers went to the same church as she, she was soon called into a meeting with the pastors. They confronted her about the rumors they'd been hearing, asking who she really was. "My response to them was, 'Well, I'm a man who used to be a woman.' And their response was, 'We love you, but we can't have you going here.'" She was promptly kicked out of the church. Yet somehow, she knew that these pastors hadn't been expressing the fullness of God's heart for her.

She continued to date other women, fully embracing her identity as a man, but she also found another church and began to read her Bible. One morning, she realized that she'd been treating her current girlfriend a lot like her dad had treated her mother. Devastated, she broke up with her and began to press into more of the Lord, getting very involved in her church.

Throughout this time, though, she developed a debilitating pornography addiction. About a year after the breakup, she was on her way to church when the Lord interrupted her thoughts, asking her if she was now ready to take an inventory of her life choices. He said to her, "Will you now? Will you now?" She thought, *I don't have anything to lose.* So, she said, "Yes. Lord, I will." Immediately, her pornography addiction just lifted. "I continued to get more and more involved in the church I was in and just made room for the Lord everywhere." As if she were a man, she was leading a men's Bible study, helping to lead junior high boys, and involved in the single adults and the college-aged group. Seeing her hunger for the Lord, the church began grooming "this young man" for leadership.

She soon connected with a couple who became her spiritual parents. One day as they were praying, she realized that they couldn't effectively pray for her when they didn't know the truth about who she was. So she told them everything. Eventually, she was called in to meet with the pastor of the church and with her spiritual dad. She prepared her heart for another confrontation, and, again, she was asked to explain who she really was. This time, though, what came out of her mouth was, "I'm a woman living as a man."

As she said that, the Holy Spirit rushed in and she immediately saw what the next steps of her journey would be: She had to step down from leadership, she had to tell the leaders in her life the truth, and she had to go back to living as a woman. Her pastor didn't know how to direct her, so instead he listened to the steps the Lord had given to her. "OK," he said, "tomorrow, give me a call, and we'll start setting up those appointments for you."

She was shocked. She thought, *You're not going to kick me out? You're not going to ask me to leave? You're going to walk with me?* As if responding to her thoughts, her pastor said, "I don't know what this is supposed to look like. I'm clueless. But I know that I will be with you in it."[1] And that changed everything for her.

Challenging the Church

In many ways, the Church has failed those who see themselves as LGBTQ. Historically avoiding the topic of sex—both the healthy expression and the dysfunctions—has left our sexuality shrouded in confusion, shame, and secrecy. In my experience, homosexuality was never discussed in church other than to vaguely reference the sin and condemnation of those who "chose" a lifestyle of homosexuality. Finding, for the most part, rules and judgment within the institution of religion, not surprisingly, those struggling with their sexual identity mostly went elsewhere for answers.

Currently, this topic is one of the most divisive among believers. But we should be mindful that much of the division occurred because the

Body of Christ dropped the ball. Too often, hurting people were disappointed when they looked to churches for encouragement. Instead of help, they were given judgment. Instead of compassion, they received shame and rejection. Instead of empathy, they were handed a lot of religious rules. Instead of tools to walk toward deep inner peace and restoration, many, many hurting people—like KathyGrace—were shown the door.

We did not love people living a homosexual lifestyle the way that Jesus would have. So, without a model of compassion and truth, many churches have decided to go the way of acceptance instead of judgment. Their hearts are loving, but they have an underweight version of love. Love without truth, love that doesn't have hope for transformation, is just as destructive as its opposite. Jesus showed us what speaking the truth in love looks like. And He calls us to do the same.

God wants to empower the Body of Christ to release healing into the sexual identity crisis the world is experiencing at this moment. We may have abdicated our position of authority in this arena because of fear and desire for control, but Jesus has called us to do more. He has poured out His Spirit on us, calling us to influence the world with Heaven's perspective. Only followers of Jesus can say to someone with full confidence, "There is hope. The Person of peace sees you and loves you unconditionally. You are forgiven by God, and you will never be alone again. Here's who God says you really are...."

When I was struggling with my sexual identity, it was my church community that came alongside me. They made room for the changes in my life, for my preferences, and for my mannerisms. There was a group of men who welcomed me into their community as merely another of the men. They accepted me completely and reinforced who I was. This is the kind of environment we can help build for others.

Wise as Serpents, Gentle as Doves

Coming alongside someone who is leaving homosexuality behind requires us to operate in both wisdom and sensitivity. Regardless of whether or not you have struggled with same-sex attraction, one of the most important first steps is to honestly evaluate what place that individual has given you in their lives. Loving and supporting someone's journey can look vastly different, depending on our relationship level. As supporters, we can ask ourselves, "Are they asking for my input into their behavior or lifestyle?" Or, alternatively, "Do we have a close enough relationship that I need to be willing to share my input, even though they may not like my counsel?"

A common analogy for understanding healthy confrontation describes relationships to be like bridges and confrontation to be like a truck. You can only drive a heavy truck over a bridge that is strong enough to carry it. Addressing someone's sexual identity is one of the heaviest "trucks" you can operate, so that relational bridge needs to be well built and stable. This means that, if your transgender co-worker asks you to use a specific pronoun, this is probably not the time to share with them the biblical truth about their lifestyle or sexual identity. We can only truly influence where we have been given access. If we overstep this boundary, we risk turning precious people—individuals who were uniquely designed in God's image—into religious projects. And if you've ever been on the receiving end of that, you know how isolating and painful it can feel.

Compassion is a huge part of creating a healing environment. Whenever I share my testimony, I'm aware that individuals in my audience may be receiving very different messages. For every person who is experiencing hope and transformation, there is another person who probably feels as if the ground just crumbled beneath him/her. Every time we share a standard, we invite comparison. This does not mean that I stop sharing God's transformation in my life. On the contrary, I'm working to reach more and more people. But it does mean that I am careful how I talk about my story. I know that I cannot prevent pain, but I can honor those who are having a different experience from me and try to minimize any pain they may feel. I do my best to bring that awareness and compassion to the forefront of my vision.

God Is Love

The truth is, even if we are doing our absolute best to show up with compassion, to build relationship, and to support those walking through this challenging process, only the Holy Spirit truly knows the way forward for each person. Each person dealing with same-sex attraction or sexual sin will need different counsel. Someone who is married to an opposite-sex spouse and is also having a same-sex adulterous affair, for example, will most likely require different boundaries—due to the lives impacted—than another person's teenage child. Compassion and love are still paramount, but dependence on the Holy Spirit to lead is everything. If we truly want to be a supportive community, we need to take a backseat to His timing. Even if we have experienced transformation in our sexuality ourselves, our story will not be the same as another person's.

Early on in KathyGrace's journey toward restoration of her identity, she had well-meaning people give her bags of makeup, encouraging her to put it on. But she wasn't ready for that. Wearing makeup would have been putting a band-aid of performance on a much deeper intimacy wound. God's goal wasn't for her to wear makeup. His goal was for her to be so secure in her identity as His daughter that she could express her femininity out of that freedom. As Drew Berryessa experienced, transformation of one's sexual identity comes from the inside out. As supporters, we need to listen to God's voice, follow His lead, and then get out of the way. Here's Drew's story:

> I lived in what felt like a secret prison of hopelessness and helplessness. I was addicted to pornography and masturbation, and I had a really hard time making friends. I also dealt with same-sex attraction and felt extremely internally conflicted and frustrated about it. I had no idea what to do with my struggles.
>
> At my lowest point, I was in despair and had no hope that things could change. I started to believe that gay love was better than no love at all, and I entered into a gay relationship. For a few months it felt fulfilling, but then I quickly realized it wasn't what others had made it out to be.
>
> Realizing that even that relationship wouldn't meet my heart's desire or satisfy me, I considered suicide. I saw no way forward, but I didn't go through with it.
>
> I wanted to have a family someday, to be married to a woman, and have kids although I honestly didn't think it would be possible for me. And I always had a deep feeling that same-sex attraction was not what was best for me. I struggled to reconcile my feelings and my faith. These were the two main motivators for me to pursue change.
>
> There were many things that helped my process, including an album of a worship leader who shared his story of coming out of homosexuality. It was the first time I'd ever

heard a testimony like it, and it gave me hope. There were also books of others' stories of leaving homosexual lifestyles that encouraged me.

I then joined a program that offered specific counseling and pastoral care for people who struggled with their sexuality. No one there was trying to coerce me into changing my behavior, but they helped me pursue a healthy heart and lifestyle, which then led me to change my behavior, as well. The people there encouraged me and helped me see who I really was. That meant letting go of the ways the rejection, abuse, and struggle had affected my view of myself.

Now I have been married for almost 15 years to my wife, and I am the father of three beautiful daughters. Those are two roles that I never thought I would be able to have. I now get to experience them every single day, and it's amazing.

I have an immense number of healthy, supportive friendships, and I have had reconciliation with each of my family members whom I felt isolated from in the past. I'm happy, successful, and excited about life.

I'm looking forward to watching my own daughters grow and eventually get married and to being a grandpa. I'm looking forward, on a really immediate level, to my youngest going to school next year so that my wife can be freed up a little bit more. Those are all the sweet little mundane things about family life that I never would have had the opportunity to look forward to had this not happened in my life.[2]

You heard in Drew's story that he was thankful no one coerced him into changing his behavior. Love is the only way forward. When we are given the honor of coming alongside someone in their journey out of homosexuality, intentionally loving choices can go a long way. Listening intently, letting him or her feel and be known, and giving of our time all express value for the person. Love means building a relationship, not preaching at someone to win an argument. It is a chance to remember that many of the roots of homosexuality are the same sources of the emotional woundedness in our lives. Whether it manifested in same-sex attraction, alcoholism, unhealthy independence, or codependency, we can all relate to the human pain that results from a breakdown of intimacy. Persons who are inviting us into their journey are giving us the precious opportunity to walk with them, to watch the Lord move mightily as the Healer and Restorer of all.

"Love does not delight in evil but rejoices with the truth" (1 Corinthians 13:6 NIV). The idea of love was never meant to be equated to mere kindness. To do so would be to reduce it greatly. Scripture takes a whole chapter of the Bible to describe this weighty concept—love. While kindness and compassion are extremely valuable, love "rejoices with the truth." Too many people have fallen into a "live and let live" mentality with regard to other people. And especially when it comes to people who are living a gay lifestyle. But that is not love.

Loving someone means to continuously ask the Lord what He is doing. Our understanding of love must be subjugated to the Person of God, not to our emotions. It is not love to stand by and watch someone damage themselves because of their own pain. Love is free from judgment, but it is right to grieve the internal reality that would be expressing itself as homosexuality. The human heart does not want to be merely tolerated. Each person desires to be seen, to be known, and to be intimately loved. And they will only receive that when they—like all of us—come face to face with Love Himself.

Free Indeed

Each one of us should live with an awareness that, by walking daily in close fellowship with the Holy Spirit and by listening for His voice, we create an environment in which God can minister to those around us. KathyGrace found this heavenly environment in her church family. So she opened her heart to God's mercy and love, and she found the complete freedom she was desiring.

> My life is very full now. I've been out of the lifestyle for 25 years. When I think back to those years of living as a man, it feels like a whole other world. I still have the memories, but it seems like I was another person.
>
> I still am a prankster and mischievous, but now I'm also free. I know who I am, and each new day is something to look forward to instead of trudge through. I now value being genuine instead of trying to hide all the time. Growing up, I was so afraid I would be rejected if I showed any emotion or anything about who I was. That was scary. Now, that's not true. Here I am; this is what you get.
>
> I got healed from so much rejection. And I understand now I'm a good person. I know I'm loved, and I find great value in life. I can't say I felt that way before. I have a confidence in who I am now and that I have value. I may not get it right all the time, but what I have to offer is good.[3]

199

After she had been living comfortably as a woman for years without experiencing same-sex attractions, she had a moment of revelation: She was totally free. While she would always continue to grow and get healthier in many ways, the battle for her identity was over. She had left same-sex attraction and sexual identity confusion behind her. Curious, she asked the Lord, "How did that happen? When did that happen? How did You change my mind because I'd made a vow that I would never go back to being a woman, and yet here I am. Lord, when did that happen?"

In her mind's eye, she saw the Lord put His hand to His chin as if He was deeply pondering her question. Finally, after a moment of silence, He looked up at her and said, "I don't know." KathyGrace was totally confused. This was God, right? Hadn't He been with her the whole time? She knew it was only because of His closeness that her freedom was even possible. So, how did He not know?

The Lord just looked at her and said, "I never saw you that way."[4]

The Life Ahead

Many in our world today are struggling and confused about who they are. But God knows exactly who we are. God didn't see Kathy-Grace as a man, He didn't see me as gay, and He told my girlfriend not to see me that way, either. The world is pushing us to go with the flow and to embrace LGBTQ ideology. But I found great freedom and fulfillment and the ability to have a family of my own by choosing to see myself as He sees me—a man of God. I think my journey took years longer than necessary because I was trying to change myself and figure it all out in my head. In reality, Father God was wanting me to lay down my methods and trust Him, lean into Him, and worship Him only. He's the only one with the power to transform us and renew our minds. My prayer is that you'll draw close enough to Him and to those He's placed in your life to receive the intimate love He has for you and to embrace and enjoy your God-given identity. All things are possible. It's worth the fight!

Notes

1. *Homosexuality and the Church: BSSM Advanced Ministry Training 2019-2020 Year,* "Session 3: What factors do transgender individuals face? With KathyGrace Duncan of Portland Fellowship," Equipped to Love.

2. Drew Berryessa, *CHANGED: #oncegay Stories,* https://changedmovement .com/stories/2018/5/28/drew-berryessa.

3. KathyGrace Duncan, *CHANGED: #oncegay Stories,* https:// changedmovement.com/stories/kathygrace-duncan.

4. *Homosexuality and the Church: BSSM Advanced Ministry Training 2019-2020 Year,* "Session 3: What factors do transgender individuals face? With KathyGrace Duncan of Portland Fellowship," Equipped to Love.

FREQUENTLY ASKED QUESTIONS

Understandably, discussing homosexuality in a faith-based setting brings up many practical issues. Below, I have consolidated some of the most frequently asked questions I have received. Despite a life of personal experience, I do not have all of the answers, but I will share my perspective along with input from several people I trust on these matters. Many of these scenarios are complex and deeply personal, and this format is tragically limited. I wish we were having a long discussion over coffee so that I could understand the full context behind the questions. However, I have tried my best to address each one with grace, compassion, and truth. My hope is that my responses will not be the final word on each topic but that they would act as a springboard as you dive deeper into the Father's heart for LGBTQ-identifying people.

Visit **CHANGEDmovement.com** and **EquippedToLove.com**
for additional resources.

1) **Q: If my child tells me that he/she thinks he/she is gay, how should I respond?**

   A: I would start by asking questions. That's a great on-ramp into the deeper things in the child's life. Ask things like: "Help me understand how you came to decide that. When was the first time you started feeling that way? Tell me about it...." The child just gave you access to the deeper things inside him; proceed gingerly. Create/provide a super safe space for him to be able to talk freely about his experiences and feelings. Remember that there are reasons that the child would say this or feel that way. So if you have a heart to help, don't focus on the outward behavior (unless the child's choices are placing him in danger); express love and grace for the inner condition (the feelings) of the child. You'll want him to know you're on his team.

   If you already have a vibrant and emotionally rich relationship, you probably have the ability to be more direct because you've built trust and your connection is strong. If your relationship isn't that strong and there's not a lot of relational collateral, you probably need to invest (empathize) and build connection and trust before you can offer much advice and expect it to be received well.

2) Q: What are things to look for in a good counselor for someone who struggles with same-sex attraction? Are there any counseling groups that you recommend?

> **A:** Of primary importance would be finding a counselor who is firmly convinced that people's sexual experience can change and that Jesus is in the business of transforming each of us into new creations. Possibly a counselor who goes to your church?
>
> Ideally, you could find someone who has experience helping people with same-sex attraction and who is connected with other counselors who have experience in this area. Choosing a counselor is very personal, but it is helpful to find someone who is patient, loving, and who will help the person feel both seen and heard.
>
> Sadly, it may be difficult to find a licensed counselor who can give counsel in line with the core values I stated because of misguided laws that are being passed in the United States and around the world. Some laws are now mandating that sexual fluidity only flow in the direction of LGBTQ, not toward heterosexuality. So people may be best helped by a pastor or minister. Also, my *Finding You: An Identity-Based Journey Out of Homosexuality and Into All Things New* course is a comprehensive discipleship program that guides the individual to draw upon the Lord, his/her church, family, and community in order to experience transformation.

3) Q: My daughter's school is having a Diversity Week to celebrate LGBTQ equality in education. As her parents, we're uncomfortable with the content that will be introduced throughout this event. Aside from pulling her out of school that week, how do we reflect the heart of the Father without compromising truth?

A: This scenario is a wonderful example of why it is best to be proactive in laying the foundation of healthy family and sexuality with your kids before they enter school. Pulling our kids out of school for this week won't shield them from encountering LGBTQ issues. Leading open discussions about sexuality, family, and male/female roles within the home when your children are very young (ideally starting by three or four years old) can frame discussions they're having or hearing at school in the context of biblical truth. Focus on loving and caring for other children who may be impacted by LGBTQ with Jesus' heart so that your children will learn to do the same.

If you're concerned about the curriculum being taught to your children, protesting Diversity Week might or might not be a fruitful place to start. But if you don't voice your concerns to school administration, it's likely that your desires to protect your children won't be accomplished. The coming Diversity Week should be a great motivation for you and your friends to begin having a presence at school board meetings. Gather like-minded parents and start building relationships with the administrators. Make sure you have a strong, consistent voice about all aspects of the schooling experience, including the curriculum.

4)   Q: Our church wants to start ministering to the LGBTQ community, but we've never been trained on how to do so. Where do you recommend we start?

A: Elizabeth Woning and I established Equipped to Love to help equip the church to deal with these types of issues. It's wonderful to hear about people's hearts to love and minister to individuals coming out of—or actively involved in—an LGBTQ lifestyle. However, before forward motion happens, I would encourage any church who is interested in engaging in this ministry to step back and honestly evaluate themselves in a few areas. First, I would ask the church if the topic of sexuality was being addressed openly and honestly from the pulpit with the larger congregation. Second, what kind of ministry is currently available for people within your own congregation to help them walk out of sexual sin? Before ministering to those within the LGBTQ subculture, it's important to build a foundation within your church of dialogue surrounding the topics of both healthy sexuality and the broad array of sexual issues.

Providing this type of open, honest teaching about these historically taboo topics can create open doors for reaching out to individuals who have left behind homosexuality or who are still involved. Who in your congregation is gay-identifying or leaving behind that lifestyle? Walk alongside them and learn how to support them on their journey. Once you understand how to address their issues, once that discipleship is already happening at the one-on-one level with people who are already a part of your church, once you can communicate the truth in love to people who identify as gay, you can begin to create safe spaces where dialogue and learning can happen.

Recognize, though, that if you begin to minister in this area you are inviting people who may not share the same core beliefs as the rest of your members. If that level of messy vulnerability would be met with fear by your congregation, your church may not yet be ready to proactively minister to those within the LGBTQ subculture. You might consider finding an active, thriving ministry that your church can partner with and support in this arena while you equip your church to minister directly.

5) **Q: Do you have any advice about introducing the issue of homosexuality to my children?**

A: Here is some counsel my wife, Tiffany, shared in her blog, "How to Talk to Your Kids About Homosexuality," that she wrote for Moral Revolution:

Let's start talking about it. A lot. The world is talking about LGBTQ everywhere we look—so why aren't we? Let's talk about God's design for family with our kids. Let's talk about His heart for those within the LGBTQ community when our kids are young—before they ever meet a gay-identified person. Let's discuss words like "gay," "lesbian," and "transgender" over the dinner table. Let's stop holding a shield in front of our kids, keeping them from these conversations and, instead, let's equip them to wield the powerful weapons of loving truth and radical compassion to the hurting people of their generation.

When we're discussing this topic with children, we can introduce age-appropriate content, prioritize listening to our kids, keeping the topic casual and low-stakes, and modeling kindness without diluting the truth. One of the answers for a hurting gay community is the intimate love of Jesus, especially through the hands and feet of His church. Sadly, the church has mostly been known for throwing stones at them. But our kids' generation could be the ones to turn the tide, building a bridge for the gay community to access the love of Jesus through His Church. This will not happen by our preaching at them, but by demonstrating a loving Christ while still upholding our values.[1]

Remember this: We tend to believe whatever we hear first. So begin talking about God's special design for family structure—a mommy and a daddy—and their unique roles and contributions *before* your kids are introduced to LGBTQ online or at school or anywhere else.

6)   **Q: My transgender daughter requested that we use only masculine pronouns when referring to her in conversation. We want to honor her but we feel this is empowering a false identity. What is the appropriate response?**

A: First, it is important to acknowledge that when someone identifies as a different sex than their biology, it represents a deep pain and confusion that may have been present for years. Because of that, much of my advice to you would depend on the depth of relationship between you and your daughter. If she feels as though you are on opposite teams, there will be a limit to how much influence you will have on her choices. However, if the relationship has remained open, there may be more of a chance for dialogue on these matters.

It is important for parents to not validate a false identity. It is perhaps even more important, though, to acknowledge that, for those individuals who are wrestling with their sexual identities, the rate of suicide is much higher than for even those dealing with same-sex attraction. This decision must be made carefully in tandem with the Holy Spirit and pastoral care, particularly if your pastor knows your family well. And regardless of the choices you make, remember that prayer is your strongest weapon. I know many stories of supernatural rescue that came in response to parents' prayers.

Also, see the answers to questions number 1 and 4.

7) Q: I often hear people say, "Isn't all sin equal?" Is homosexuality a bigger deal than gluttony, worshiping money, adultery, etc.? If so, why?

A: All sin is equal in the sense that every sin separates us from God and requires Jesus' sacrifice to reconcile us to the perfect Father. It is important to recognize, though, that the Bible says sexual sin damages the person's own body (see 1 Corinthians 6:18). Because it is so deeply intimate and relational, sexual sin impacts not only our own selves but also our ability to connect to others as well as our capacity for intimacy with God.

People who commit sexual sin are not necessarily more evil than those who commit other sins. We have all sinned and fallen short of God's glory (see Romans 3:23). But it does us good to be sober about the harm—physically, psychologically, and spiritually—that sexual sin brings on ourselves, on others, and potentially on future generations. Because LGBTQ lifestyles directly upset God's design for family structure—husband and wife leading sons and daughters—the effects can be intense and far-reaching.

8) **Q: Do you think it's important to remove someone from a leadership role in the church if they came out as LGBTQ?**

A: Yes, I do. But how this is done can be the difference between alienating and further wounding hurting persons and discipling them toward freedom and wholeness. Because the Church is so new at addressing sexual issues openly, it is important to handle confrontations like this lovingly and graciously. It helps greatly if there are pre-existing guidelines/requirements for church leadership that can be referenced. But any conversation of this nature needs to start with compassionate questions instead of accusations and within a private and appropriate setting.

The person needs to experience that your focus is on his/her well-being rather than on the church's liability or fear. Try to understand where the person is coming from, and see if they are open to help. But communicate clearly your expectations for those in leadership roles within the church. Reiterate your desire to maintain relationship with them, keeping concern for the individual at the forefront, but communicate that their choice to pursue a lifestyle which includes sexual behavior that does not align with biblical scripture goes against the expectations the church has for anyone in a leadership role. Explain that anyone not adhering to the biblical qualifications of church leadership would need to step down until they could return to that standard (see 1 Timothy 3:1-15).

Elizabeth Woning likes to point out that ideally church leadership proactively develops a relationship with any LGBTQ-identified persons soon after they begin attending the church. Strive to be transparent regarding doctrine and teaching. It is painful when rules or standards get enforced years after a person has been involved in your fellowship. Sharing those standards earlier as a normal part of the discipleship process, though sometimes challenging, is more honoring and probably more Christlike.

9) **Q: Can you be gay and a Christian?**

A: God does not give the identity of "gay." So you can be experiencing same-sex attraction and be a Christian, yes. There are also many stories of people who met the Lord but spent years building relationship with Him before He seemed to specifically address their sexuality. He's concerned with our hearts in addition to our behavior.

If someone said that he/she was gay, I would first wonder what that meant to him/her. If that means that he/she experiences same-sex attraction, but he/she is refraining from engaging in homosexual sex, then certainly that person can be following Christ. If the person has owned the gay identity and is living a celibate life, I'd be sad that he/

she owned an identity ("gay Christian") that God didn't give to him/her, but I can see how this person could be a true Christ follower. Just because a person doesn't have hope for his/her sexual desires to change does not disqualify him/her from being *in Christ*.

However, if a person has fully embraced living a homosexual identity *and* a lifestyle of sexual sin, then I would have concern as to whether the person is a true follower of Christ, because Christ is never going to lead people in a direction contrary to the Bible's instruction. Any time we question whether a person genuinely knows the Lord, it is wise to pray and ask Father God what He is doing inside of the person and align our prayers and actions with that. Jesus, for example, only did what He saw His Father doing (see John 5:19-20).

10) **Q: What wisdom or advice would you give to parents of children who are expressing a desire to be the opposite sex? Or, for example, to parents who have a young male child who is showing more "feminine" tendencies?**

   A: First, please read the answers to questions 1 and 6 above.

   Because I believe homosexual or transgender tendencies are most often a manifestation of intimacy breakdowns for the child in question, I would encourage the parents to pray consistently and ask Father God what He is doing in the child's life. Understanding what God's priorities are for this season of the boy's life will be very helpful. The Holy

Spirit knows what the boy needs. Also, focus on ensuring that the child feels truly seen, heard, and safe to communicate how he feels.

Rather than trying to get the boy *not* to play with dolls, in most cases I would suggest requesting to *join* your boy in his play and trying to connect with him there. Figure out what he most enjoys playing with and ask him what he likes about it. This will strengthen your relational connection and probably heighten his appreciation for you. You may eventually be able to invite your son into some new activities that could be done together with same-sex members of his family or friends. Attention and affirmation should be applied liberally, particularly by the same-sex parent (or a trusted, same-sex role model). And statistically, there is a good likelihood that the child will outgrow any sense of gender dysphoria.

Ideally, the child will be able to begin to build relationships with same-sex peers, will bond with the same-sex parent (or a trusted, same-sex role model) and begin to esteem and embrace his own biological sex.

11) **Q: My female cousin is marrying a woman this summer. I want to show her how much I love her, but I also don't want to compromise what my faith tells me about same-sex marriage. What should I do?**

A: There are underlying, emotional reasons why your cousin has chosen to marry another woman. So, whatever you decide—and how you communicate that decision—must

include the gentle compassion that comes with the awareness of the complexity of pain that undergirds her choice.
There are many leaders I love and respect greatly who
would draw a hard line and say that under no circumstances is it righteous to attend a gay wedding.

The reasons not to attend are sound and often right: It is
difficult to attend without condoning the marriage, there
may be people watching your decision who will be confused and/or influenced by your attendance, the Bible
does not condone same-sex marriage ever. These are
absolutely true, and if your relationship is a fairly distant
one it might be easy to bow out of the ceremony without
any relational damage. However, if this is a close relationship, I think it is valuable to weigh the relational context
when making this challenging decision.

The risk of attending, in this scenario, would be potentially
appearing to condone the same-sex union. The risk of
refusing might be to send a message of rejection to someone you are called to love, limiting your ability to reach
him/her. This is a moment when our reliance on the Holy
Spirit is paramount. Ideally, if this is a close relationship,
no matter what you decide, there would have been consistent, open dialogue prior to the wedding invitation. This
might look like you listening to your cousin's heart and
her reasons for coming out as gay while you share God's
absolute love for her along with the truth that you don't
think this is God's best for her life. If that honest exchange
of perspectives has already taken place, you can openly
share your objection to attending the wedding along with
your unwavering love and support for her.

I imagine a dialogue going something like this: "Julie, you know that I will continue to be strongly in your life and fighting for your happiness for as long as I am alive. You know I believe that this is not God's best plan for your life. I have decided to (do) _____ because of my conviction about _____. My love for you is _____. You can count on me to do/be _____ going forward."

Obviously, it would be inappropriate to have a scripted conversation. But sometimes you just need to have a kind but frank conversation and plainly state the truth—that both parties would prefer that the other party would see things differently, but, for the sake of the relationship, both parties need to be willing to give some grace to the other party and not demand that the other party changes in order to continue the relationship.

12) **Q: Do you think it's important for Christians to politically oppose the legalization of same-sex marriage? If so, why, if it most often relates to people who don't share our Christian belief system anyway? Isn't that just an example of the separation of Church and State?**

   A: I absolutely understand why many Christians think that we are not called to force our beliefs on others through the political realm. I agree that it is not our job to coerce people who do not have a relationship with God to behave like Christians. After all, there were two types of trees in the garden of Eden. God gave Adam and Eve choices. However, I am against the legalization of same-sex marriage because I believe that such a ruling leaves behind innocent victims.

As I discussed in Chapter 3, children of same-sex families do not get to experience a home life covered by both biological sexes as God intended. In the big picture, the very fabric of our culture is founded upon the institution of family. It's at the core of our society. When you begin to disintegrate or change the shape of that building block—removing the feminine or the masculine covering from the family unit—the effects are incalculable. The institution of marriage is sacred and worthy of protecting politically, socially, and spiritually.

13) **Q: The LGBTQ community seems to be constantly pushing their agenda forward. How are Christians supposed to advance or speak truth without picketing and coming across as hateful?**

> **A:** As Christians, we get our direction from God. Like Jesus, we are called to only do what our Father does and only say what our Father says (see John 8:28). If we start to get our marching orders in reaction to what the world is doing, the ugliest side of religion can emerge. Our concern, then, needs to be whether we are obeying the Lord in our own lives rather than whether other people are obeying Him in theirs. Not everyone shares our beliefs or core values.
>
> But if God is leading us to speak out on an issue like the LGBTQ agenda, we need to make sure compassion and love, in addition to a conviction for righteousness, are

leading the way. We will only have the influence to bring life and breakthrough into an arena where we can lead with love. And oftentimes, those who have the easiest access to compassion in this area are those who came out of the homosexual experience. Supporting ministries like CHANGED Movement, run by individuals who have left the LGBTQ identity behind them and are now empowering others, is a powerful way to lend our strength.

But with all of that said, be proactive. Work to vote righteous leaders into government. Take responsibility for the health of your city. Pray for your leaders and for God to have His way in your midst. And do everything He is leading you to do; just maybe check with others in your life before doing something public or on social media. There is safety in a multitude of counselors (see Proverbs 11:14).

14) Q: There are verses in the Old Testament that say homosexuality is wrong, but there are also verses denouncing tattoos, pork, and shellfish. Why is homosexuality not accepted by contemporary Christians in the same way tattoos and bacon are?

A: Elizabeth Woning has shared her thoughts below:

Through the Mosaic covenant, including all its accompanying behavioral restrictions, God was creating a new cultural identity for the descendants of Abraham, Isaac, and Jacob. Remember, they had just left Egypt after being there 430 years! Many Christians read the Torah and are baffled by the sheer number of lifestyle requirements essential to

Jewish identity. It's vital to understand that these laws were applied differently and had varying levels of penalties. Some requirements focused upon rituals for worship and the priesthood, and others for social and personal relationships. Therefore, some had moral and even symbolic significance (revealing God's nature in understandable ways), while others were similar to federal or state laws such as the speed limit. God was legislating accepted practices among neighbors, tribes, cities, and nations as well as moral attitudes. And so, it's inappropriate to equate "eating bacon" to sexual immorality, such as rape, adultery, or homosexuality.

When we read the Old Testament, it's helpful to identify the different extremes in the administration of justice according to Torah law. An "unclean" person who has touched a dead body need only undergo a washing ritual to be restored to communal favor (see Numbers 19:11-12). That's not much of a penalty. Food restrictions relate to health issues (for example, swine and shrimp are scavengers). The logic behind these practices is obvious. Similarly, adultery and murder have extreme penalties (death) as a consequence to the impact on broader social relationships. Consider that Moses lists homosexual *behavior* (not identity) among infractions that warrant the death penalty. That suggests that homosexual practice has drastic personal and cultural implications according to God.

This is important to consider as we empower different behaviors within Christian fellowship. The Bible indicates that sexual behaviors have deep significance to God because they impact a person's body (the promised dwelling place

219

of God's Spirit) and our relationships together. There is no place in Scripture in which God blesses same-sex sexual unions; therefore, it is important that we align ourselves with His values. When we experience same-sex attraction or sexual identity confusion as disciples of Jesus, we can be confident that God promises to bring us into alignment with His values.

15) **Q: What would you say is the best way to reach out to those in a homosexual lifestyle and attempt to minister to them when they appear to be content with their lifestyle?**

A: Be full of the Holy Spirit and be prepared to listen to what He wants to share with those persons. Most likely, this will not mean discussing their behavior or lifestyle unless you have been in deep, long-term relationship with them. Many people who have come out of the LGBTQ subculture have done so because they have tasted the radical, overwhelming love of God that met them in the midst of their lifestyle. I have many formerly LGBTQ friends who found Jesus as a result of a word of knowledge, a prophetic word, or through some supernatural event from God. So the best way to reach out is through Spirit-led ministry, love, and encouragement. Just be sure that you are reaching out because of your love for the individual, not because you are preoccupied with their behavior.

Experiencing God, the one who pursues them to offer His love in the midst of their mess, is what truly changes people's lives. Romans says, *"The kindness of God leads you to repentance*" (Romans 2:4 NASB). So we want to be full of God ourselves and, therefore, representing Him well long before we address behavior. It's not our job to be the Holy Spirit, but to be led by Him.

16) **Q: How do I support a friend who has been labeled as gay (by society or peers) because of his appearance and mannerisms? Where do stereotypical gay mannerisms come from? Are they learned or inborn?**

A: So often, as a society, we can focus on someone's outward appearance and assume we know what's going on inside of them. For someone who is effeminate or perhaps tomboyish, the judgmental messages they receive about their identity can be debilitating and alienating. So the first advice I would give is to just come alongside that person. Jesus didn't come to condemn people; He cared for them and invited them into relationship with Him.

We can show compassion for a person's pain, becoming a safe place for him/her to process. Much harm has been done when individuals who have different mannerisms feel as if there is no grace or understanding for them and no place for them to fit in with the rest of culture. It only serves to push them further into isolation.

The late, great Sy Rogers explained that stereotypically gay mannerisms are like having an accent. Our mannerisms are influenced by those we're surrounded by and those we desire to emulate. In that way, we are products of our environment, but God bypasses all of our self-constructs and goes straight to the heart. In this way, and every way, we can follow His lead.

Note

1. For age-appropriate discussion prompts, or to read the full article written by Tiffany Williams: https://www.moralrevolution.com/blog/how-to-talk -to-your-kids-about-homosexuality.

RECOMMENDED RESOURCES

Featured Resources (visit EquippedToLove.com or CHANGEDmovement.com):

- *Finding You: An Identity-Based Journey Out of Homosexuality and Into All Things New* online course by Ken Williams
- *Pastoring Homosexuality* e-course by Elizabeth Woning
- *CHANGED: #oncegay Stories* (book of testimonies)

Featured Websites (visit Resources pages):

- EquippedToLove.com
- CHANGEDmovement.com
- MoralRevolution.com
- KenWilliamsMinistries.com

Understanding Homosexuality

- *The Broken Image: Restoring Personal Wholeness Through Healing Prayer* by Leanne Payne
- *Pursuing Sexual Wholeness: How Jesus Heals the Homosexual* by Andrew Comiskey
- *The Bible and Homosexual Practice: Texts and Hermeneutics* by Dr. Robert A.J. Gagnon
- *God and Sexuality: Truth and Relevance Without Compromise* by Janet Boynes

Intimacy Journey

- *Good Morning, Holy Spirit* by Benny Hinn
- *The Shack* by William Paul Young

Experiencing God's Presence

- *When Heaven Invades Earth: A Practical Guide to a Life of Miracles* by Bill Johnson

Renewing the Mind

- *The Supernatural Power of the Transformed Mind: Access to a Life of Miracles* by Bill Johnson
- *Battlefield of the Mind: Winning the Battle in Your Mind* by Joyce Meyer
- *Victorious Emotions* by Wendy Backlund

Hearing God

- *You Can Hear the Voice of God: How God Speaks in Listening Prayer* by Steve Sampson
- *Listening Prayer: Learning to Hear God's Voice and Keep a Prayer Journal* by Leanne Payne

Spirit-led Community

- *ManAlive: The Making of Men* by Mark Peterson
- *Unpunishable: Ending Our Love Affair with Punishment* by Danny Silk

Inner Healing

- *The Bondage Breaker* by Neil Anderson
- *Shifting Atmospheres: Discerning and Displacing the Spiritual Forces Around You* by Dawna De Silva
- *Winning the War Within: The Journey to Healing and Wholeness* by Jason Vallotton
- *Spirit Wars: Winning the Invisible Battle Against Sin and the Enemy* by Kris Vallotton

Vulnerability

- *Strength in Weakness: Healing Sexual and Relational Brokenness* by Andrew Comiskey
- *Daring Greatly: How the Courage to Be Vulnerable Transforms the Way We Live, Love, Parent, and Lead* by Dr. Brené Brown

Surrender

- *Breaking Free: Understanding Sexual Addiction and the Healing Power of Jesus* by Russell Willingham
- CovenantEyes.com monitoring software
- ConquerSeries.com group curriculum
- *Porn Free* online course by John Bevere

Relationships

- *The Father Heart of God: Experiencing the Depths of His Love for You* by Floyd McClung, Jr.
- *Experiencing Father's Embrace* by Jack Frost
- *Fathered by God: Learning What Your Dad Could Never Teach You* by John Eldredge
- *Codependent No More: How to Stop Controlling Others and Start Caring for Yourself* by Melody Beattie
- *Boundaries* by Dr. Henry Cloud

Identity

- *Identity Restoration: Know, Believe, and Live the Truth of Who You Are* by Ray Leight
- *Who Do You Think You Are?: An In-Depth Study of Your Identity in Christ* by Ray Leight
- *Fashioned to Reign: Empowering Women to Fulfill Their Divine Destiny* by Kris Vallotton (women's issues)
- *Powerful and Free: Confronting the Glass Ceiling for Women in the Church* by Danny Silk (women's issues)
- *All Things New: A Former Lesbian's Lifelong Search for Love* by Debora Barr (women's issues)

- *Restoring Sexual Identity: Hope for Women Who Struggle with Same-Sex Attraction* by Anne Paulk (women's issues)

- *Wild at Heart: Discovering the Secret of a Man's Soul* by John Eldredge (men's issues)

- *Crisis in Masculinity* by Leanne Payne (men's issues)

- *Desires in Conflict: Hope for Men Who Struggle with Sexual Identity* by Joe Dallas (men's issues)

- *For Such a Time* by Jeffrey McCall (gender confusion issues)

- *Understanding Gender Confusion: A Faith Based Perspective* by Denise Shick (gender confusion issues)

Enduring Faith

- *Igniting Faith in 40 Days: The Power of Hope, Declarations, and Negativity Fasts* by Steve Backlund

- *Strengthen Yourself in the Lord: How to Release the Hidden Power of God in Your Life* by Bill Johnson

Vision

- *The Purpose-Driven Life: What on Earth Am I Here for?* by Rick Warren

- *The Believer's Authority* by Kenneth Hagin

- *Are We There Yet?: Sexuality, the Church, and the Road to Transformation* by Drew Berryessa
- *The God of My Parents: The Uncensored Account of My Journey to Find Identity* by Liz Flaherty

ABOUT KEN WILLIAMS

Ken Williams began a pursuit of his true sexual identity in 1987 when his battle against homosexuality grew into intentions of suicide. During the following years, he gave himself to desperate prayer, counseling, and research. Eventually, Ken began to experience God's involvement in his journey and received healing of trauma, forged deep intimacy with God, and established masculine identity. Today, Ken helps others find genuine identity and pursue resolution of sexual issues. Ken is a co-founder of Equipped to Love, a ministry to those impacted by LGBTQ (EquippedToLove.com); is co-founder of the CHANGED Movement, a growing, grass-roots movement of men and women who no longer find identity in LGBTQ (CHANGEDmovement .com); has been an associate pastor at Bethel Church (Redding, California) since 2006; ministers and teaches on behalf of Moral Revolution (moralrevolution.com); and holds a B.S. in Marketing/Finance. His greatest joys are his beautiful wife and their four incredible children.